THE ZEN WAY

First published by Sheldon Press 1977
Second edition published by the Zen Centre 1987
Third edition published by the Buddhist Society Trust 2021

ISBN 978 0 901032 60 7

Printed in the UK

Published by
THE BUDDHIST SOCIETY
58 Eccleston Square
London, SW1V 1PH
T: 020 7834 5858
E: info@thebuddhistsociety.org
www.thebuddhistsociety.org

A catalogue record of this book is available from the British Library

Text, Translation and Commentary by the Venerable Myokyo-ni

Cover design by Robert & Gail Marcuson
Edited by Carenza Parker
Designed by Avni Patel

In association with
THE ZEN CENTRE
58 Marlborough Place
London, NW8 1PH
E: shoboan_zen_centre@yahoo.co.uk
rinzaizencentre.org.uk

THE ZEN WAY

Venerable Myokyo-ni

THE
ZEN
CENTRE

THE BUDDHIST SOCIETY TRUST

CONTENTS

FOREWORD

In 1972, Irmgard Schloegl returned to London after 12 years training in Japan under two great Zen masters, Sesso Soho Roshi and Sojun Kannun Roshi. A group of students at the Buddhist Society, many quite young, soon grew up around her. All were full of enthusiasm and eager to learn about this mysterious thing called Zen, up to then known only in the abstract from books.

Without any of the traditional trappings of a Zen teacher, this quite homely-looking woman was possessed of an inner strength and a depth of insight which commanded instant respect. Her eyes were quick and lively, and if you dared to look into them, completely enigmatic; they seemed to be bottomless and nothing came back. Her voice could be full of warmth when you brought her your troubles, or her words sharp as a knife when you acted out. A verse from the Bull-Herding poem's comes to mind. When the liberated one "returns to the marketplace", it is said, *'Bare-chested and bare-footed he enters the market, face streaked with dust and head covered with ashes. But a mighty laugh spreads from cheek to cheek. Without humbling himself to perform miracles, suddenly dead trees burst into bloom.'* Those who knew Irmgard Schloegl fresh from Japan will agree with this sentiment.

For many years, Irmgard remained a lay practitioner. But one day she said, 'I am going to ordain.' I was shocked, and couldn't help blurting out, 'But what about us, what about the group?' She said, very kindly, 'It won't make any difference at all. And frankly if it did, I wouldn't do it.' I was deeply moved and have never forgotten it. The idea that she would readily have foregone ordination – which she dearly wanted – for the sake of her students was immensely humbling. To have such a teacher is a blessing.

Irmgard's ordination took place at Chithurst monastery in West Sussex, in the presence of the monastic community and invited lay people. It was a warm summer's day, and Soko Roshi and his monks came from Japan to conduct the ceremony. They chanted the names of the masters in the line of transmission, beginning with the seven legendary Buddhas, and the Buddha of our era, Sakyamuni, through the line of Indian and Chinese patriarchs and the Chinese and Japanese Zen masters up to Sesso Soho Roshi who was Irmgard's first teacher.

It was a reminder that the Zen teachings have come down to us from the Buddha. With this ceremony, Irmgard became the Venerable Myokyo-ni (Mirror of the Subtle). And as she promised, her ordination made no difference. Except, well, there was one thing. She said smilingly, 'I am no longer allowed to hug the boys.'

Initially, we students were strongly discouraged from reading about Zen. Our heads were too full of what she called our 'fancy ideas.' Zen training as she constantly reminded us is largely physical. Soko Morinaga Roshi, who was the head monk at Daitoku-ji monastery when Myokyo-ni first arrived, told us, 'When I heard that Dr Schloegl was coming, I thought "Oh no, not another western academic." But I was mistaken. She already understood that Zen is in the body, not in the head.'

The Zen Way was published in 1977, and became the standard text for Zen Centre trainees. It remains so to this day: such books never date. The Venerable Myokyo-ni died in 2007. Her posthumous name, as chanted in the line of transmission, is Daiku Myokyo Zenji ('Zen Master Great Oak'). Shortly before her death she remarked, 'The forms do not matter. What matters is that the Dharma continues.' Master Daiyu is no longer here. But her teachings remain, and those inclined to explore them will find them in this book.

I write this foreword in deep gratitude to Master Daiyu, to her two teachers Sesso Roshi and Kannun Roshi, and to the fellow students alongside whom I have been so fortunate to train. The Way which she found in Japan and brought back to England is not hers alone, nor does it belong to her direct students; it belongs to all who wish to follow it. I hope that this new edition of *The Zen Way* will reach another generation of seekers, and inspire them to follow the Way she walked, and which she taught us to love.

Garry Gelade
London 2019

INTRODUCTION

The Zen Way is a Buddhist Way, and as such it is the Buddha's Way. Buddhism is one of the great religions, but it differs fundamentally from our Western religions. Indeed, in the light of those, it seems not to be a religion at all.

The best approach to Buddhism is to be clear about the fundamental assumptions of our own religion and of our cultural background which is conditioned by it, and has to a great extent shaped our way of thinking.

Christianity, Judaism and Islam are 'book' religions; that is, their tenets and dogmas were revealed once and for all by the divinity who is also the sole creator of all that is, and who transcends his creation, is apart from it. Approach to him, salvation by him, is only possible by perfect obedience to his commandments and belief in the dogmas he revealed, which constitute 'the book'. He can save his creatures or everlastingly damn them beyond redress.

Such assumptions are foreign to Buddhism and indeed to all Eastern systems. Whatever their dogmatic formulations, there is no sole and omnipotent creator god who can save or damn any man for ever. Nor is there any need for such a god in the Eastern religions which assume an impersonal universal law, inherent in all things. This law has all the attributes of divinity, but is immutable, not personalised as in the theistic religions; not being apart from created, manifested things, it is their principle or nature; it does not antedate them, has not created them; it does not *do* anything – it *is*!

The Buddha, however he was mythologised as the personi-fication of the principle of awakening, was a human being, a man who by his own efforts awakened from the illusions of our unquestioned and incorrect assumptions as from a dream, and who spent the rest of his life teaching that Way to all who wished to follow him.

What, then, are the basic tenets of the Buddha's Way? Nothing is permanent; what has a beginning is also bound to come to an end. Though this is obvious to us as a statement of fact, emotionally we reject it; we wish for what we like and, should we get it, cling to it and will not let it go, or we react against what we do not like as if it were permanent rather than passing. Nor does this pertain to objects only, but also to people and to views, opinions and ideals. Since we cannot always have our way, in fact usually do not, we are full of woe, wishing for what we have not and rejecting what we have. In short, we live subjectively in an illusory world of our own making, driving hither and thither, and mostly not liking it. The real trouble-maker, says the Buddha, is I myself, the selfish I that clings to my will, my wish, as I like it, as I want it, what I cannot bear, the whole gamut that I throws up. The Buddha says that this I is at best a memory chain; in itself, it is unreal, non-existent. To illustrate this he uses the analogy of the chariot, which is neither the body of the carriage, nor the wheels, nor the axle, but a complex of these parts conveniently labelled chariot; apart from its components correctly assembled there is no such thing.

The Buddhist Way, the training in Buddhism, consists mainly of breaking up I into its component parts and reas-sembling them in a manner that comes closer to what is truly human.

Why this is of paramount importance may be seen in the analogy of the Wheel of Being on which we are said to whirl, bound upon it by ourselves, thus also able to obtain release from it. This release is what the Buddha taught; it has been his message through the ages. It is achieved not by just believing in what he said, for that is of no avail, but by following his example, and ourselves treading the Way he showed.

Doctrinally this Wheel of Being is divided and consists of six distinct realms. The population of those is not permanent; residence in them is taken up as the result of volitional actions. When the energy of this link-up is exhausted, a pull exerts itself that shunts into a now better-fitting state. This may be taken as lasting for whole life-spans, or may also be for momentary states. A 'high' of heavenly feeling exhausts itself, and is replaced by a corresponding 'low' of misery, for example. Thus we whirl upon that wheel endlessly – or seemingly so. The process is self-regulating, and needs no higher authority that rewards or punishes. The law is, and one is sole master of one's fate, with nobody to blame but oneself, and nobody to help one on that Way but one's own sustained effort.

Though this may seem hard and cold to somebody reared in the belief of a loving father, warmth is not lacking in Buddhism. Visits to Buddhist countries easily show at least a surface level of piety, and it is embodied in the great teachers of Buddhism. For though the law is impersonal and indeed must be so, the appellation 'All-Compassionate One' for the Buddha illustrates our gratitude, warmth, love for having shown us the Way of release from that Wheel, and the joy that comes from it.

The heavenly realm of the Wheel is inhabited by god-like beings; but even during their tenure of it they are not omnipotent and one of the things they cannot do is to bring any man to his awakening. This is understandable, for they are themselves not awakened, merely in a very pleasant phase upon the Wheel. By definition the Buddha is their teacher as well as the teacher of men, and together with all that is, they rejoice whenever a man awakens. For it is only from the state of man that liberation from the Wheel, awakening, can take place. Hence the importance of the state of man, and the responsibility it carries. From the third state, that of dumb animals, only change is possible, not release. Whatever suffering comes their way, they have to endure it without redress. Suffering reaches its peak in the miserable realm often designated as hell with constant torture and no respite. Then there is the realm of the Hungry Ghosts whose very constitution is so that their exorbitant greed cannot be satisfied. And finally there is the realm of the Fighting Demons, mighty but violent spirits in an almost constant state of rage.

If this conception of the Wheel of Being is compared with one of the fundamental Buddhist tenets, the Three Fires – that is, desire, anger and delusion – it begins to make sense in an almost frightening way. Do we not all know these states, transmigrating through them ceaselessly day by day, and in our dreams at night? Do we not long for peace, or happiness, in short for release, for warmth, for fulfilment? This is what beckons as the aim of the Buddha's Way.

To realise this, the Buddha taught the Four Noble Truths, which are suffering, the cause of suffering, that this cause can be brought to an end, and the Way that leads to that end, called The Noble Eightfold Path. Another way of expressing this is that life is full of woe, disease of mind and body because of the basic delusion which makes it impossible for us to see things as they are. However, what has a cause can also be remedied by working out that cause, and thus release, awakening, is possible and may be found by means of treading The Noble Eightfold Path as taught by the Buddha.

Buddhism is a widely travelled religion; lacking a supreme and jealous god, it has always accommodated itself to the cultural values of its host countries and in time refined them though keeping the local characteristics. This makes for the wide variety of expression which is the first thing that meets the eye when travelling in Buddhist countries, together with the piety of the believers. It cannot be stressed too much that the structural form of Buddhism grew in various countries serving life styles culturally different from our own, and is the product of centuries of development and mutual interaction with those cultures. As a form, it cannot be imported.

Thus Buddhism is a vast conglomeration of scriptures, teachings, commentaries, traditionally inflected by the culture of countries where it has long been established. It is very much a living religion. As such, it serves two ends. In its ecclesiastical structure, its temples and shrines and the monks' traditional service to the community, it helps the believer to find meaning and purpose in his life, to be reconciled to his lot, and as a responsible individual to take his part in the community.

However, there is another side to religion, perhaps more pronounced in Buddhism than in any other, that of release. Release from the Wheel, release from any I-wrought bondage, release from I with its perpetual wants and hates that make up our misery.

Though the main stages of this way are constant in all ages and times, they have also become overlaid by the religion and culture in which they function. These constitute the trappings to render the Way perceptible within the religious and cultural context. When the religious and cultural values to which they pertain become obsolete, the trappings tend to become rigid and are mistaken for the Way itself. Just as a way that is not walked upon soon loses the features of a way and returns to the surrounding countryside with possibly a few vestiges remaining.

We in the West, having squandered our own spiritual inheritance, are compelled to look for a replacement. For whether we know it or not, we need to fill the inner hollowness with something, some seeming value – or it fills itself with some archaic eruption from within, or fastens on to some trendy-ism. Nature abhors a vacuum, and the heart longs for its fulfilment. Fulfilment, however, is something quite different from zealous enthusiasm, or from merely having one's way.

In fulfilment, both the heart and the mind are content, the break between heart and mind, between reason and emotions, is healed. What this means subjectively is a matter of experience. Abstractly, it can be said that in it, depth of understanding or Wisdom, and warmth of heart or Love, balance each other in scope and depth, thus unlocking the very source of creative energy to function freely but tempered by love and wisdom. The primal emotional energy has been transformed, and has thus become truly humanised in the best sense of the word.

Primal energy as such is primitive, non-human. If it is not tempered, it flares up as enthusiasm or hate – they turn easily into each other. Though this energy engages the whole of us and accordingly we long for it, we also fear it because it rushes us irresistibly into actions we could never perpetrate in cold blood; though it can also act creatively, it is always shortsighted if not downright blind, and our religious and political history is an object-lesson of what its destructive aspect is capable of.

It is of the greatest importance to be quite clear about this difference. The energy is the same. The tempering of it into Love and Wisdom sloughs off its destructive aspect. This can be achieved only by individual effort which brings about a valid change of heart.

This heart is our human heart; not as the physical organ, but as used in expressions like 'a kind heart', or 'my heart pounded' (as with some emotion), or 'my heart stood still' (as with shock), also in connection with deep-seated convictions such as 'I feel it in my heart'. This common usage points to 'heart' as the seat of feelings and emotions; as such, the term is used throughout.

Just as the physical organ, this heart with its feelings and emotions is common to us all. We all know only too well the tremendous strength of emotional energy. Hence the perennial emotional problems, such as falling in love, or out of it. Even common language puts these as events that befall us, often against our will and reason. Thus the way to a change of heart, or to transform the energy of the emotions, is more than I can do by an act of will. But since we all are subject to the same emotions, the way to transform their energy has common features, though doctrinal formulations differ widely.

Since this change of heart is what the Zen Way leads to, and since there is little if anything in our personal or cultural background which points directly to this all-important change, a quotation from Thomas Merton will help to show that, on the 'inner way', acquaintance with and transformation of the emotional energy is essential.

'I think that if there is one truth that people need to learn, in the world, especially today, it is this: the intellect is only theoretically independent of desire and appetite in ordinary, actual practice. It is constantly being blinded and perverted by the ends and aims of passions and the evidence it presents to us with such a show of impartiality and objectivity is fraught with interest and propaganda. We have become marvellous at self-delusion; all the more so because we have gone to such trouble to convince ourselves of our own absolute infallibility. The desires of the flesh – and by that I mean not only sinful desires, but even the ordinary, normal appetites for comfort and ease and human respect – are fruitful sources of every kind of error and misjudgement, and because we have these yearnings in us, our intellects (which, if they operated all alone in a vacuum, would indeed register with pure impartiality what they saw) present to us everything distorted and accommodated to the norms of our desire.'[1]

Language admirably expresses quite unconscious assumptions that underlie our reasoning processes, influences them, and leads them astray just because we never bothered to inquire into their tenuous grip. If we speak of the heart of the matter or accuse someone of having a cold heart we do not mean the physical organ. If 'I know something in my heart', I will not be able to keep cool should it be disparaged. The content thus held need not be concerned with truth at all; it is the emotional aspect of it that makes it compelling, robs us of our cool head, blinds us and drives us into some reaction and subsequent action.

1. Thomas Merton, *The Seven Storey Mountain* (Sheldon Press, 1978), p. 205.

Moreover, an incontrovertible truth is rarely thus held in the heart. Few people would get hot and bothered if somebody denied that the sun rises in the morning, or that it gets dark at night.

So the first insight into this matter is that it is by no means Truth as such, but MY TRUTH, which if threatened brings up in us a wild stone-age man who rushes out, face red, eyes glaring, cudgel lifted, to defend as of old 'my territory'.

This primitive wildness in our emotional reactions is as such neither good nor bad, merely purposeful. It still enables our mammalian brothers to survive, as it enabled our forebears to survive and evolve. What remained neglected in our evolutionary progress is precisely the gentling and taming of this primitive wildness of our emotions. Traditionally, we associate them with blood and heart.

We are now in a better position to understand the basic tenets of Buddhism; but more important still, we can see the crucial mistranslation of a fundamental term in Buddhism, 'heart', which until recently was always rendered as 'mind'. No other factor has contributed so much to a misunderstanding of the Buddha's message. 'Mind' by definition and connotation is the instrument of reason, of consciousness, associated with cool deliberation and I.

We can speak of a disordered mind, but never of a wild mind or a warm mind. The mind if not 'fired' from underneath by primitive or unrealised emotion, functions well of itself. The spanner in the works is the emotional factor, and that is associated with the heart, and with I.

Hence the way of deliverance is not a 'training of the mind', intellectual gymnastics or conjuring tricks, but a way of training that has as its object the transformation of primitive emotional energy, *not* sublimation which at best changes its direction, but as a genuine transformation of that energy itself. That this also constitutes a valid humanisation of this energy is obvious, and so within the Buddhist teaching of the Wheel of Being (p. 11) the human state is realised – which is both the condition of deliverance and the end of it in its developed aspect of insight-love.

In this, the little I which is the shuttlecock of the emotions, is dethroned. Or perhaps better expressed, it gives in and merges in a wholeness which is total; in losing itself in it, I is fulfilled.

This little I in its overweening self-importance causes us so much trouble. And yet, it is a mediator that cannot be dispensed with. The little I is best considered as a half-way stage; the yearning for fulfilment inherent in I would point that way. The difficulty lies in the basic misunderstanding, in Buddhism called delusion or ignorance, which is that I see fulfilment in having my way rather than in losing myself. Yet we all do the latter in moments when we are deeply moved, and just because of this we treasure such moments. We also know that at times when we are not self-conscious, our performance is 'greater'; every artist knows this well. At such times I am merged into a totality which contains the performer and the performance. In Zen language, the actor has become one with the act. The Zen Way strives towards this at-one-ment which by losing my little self, is also my fulfilment. But the losing must happen in awareness.

How this comes about will be developed in the last two chapters.

Venerable Myokyo-ni

THE BUDDHA

The man who became the Buddha was born about 2,500 years ago. His father was the king of a little Himalayan kingdom. Legend has it that a sage prophesied of the newly born heir to the throne that he would either become a mighty king and conqueror or a great sage. Since his father was naturally keen on his son and successor's career as a king he reared him carefully avoiding anything that might awaken an urge for a religious life. So we are told that the boy was brought up in the lap of luxury, strictly kept within the bounds of the palace, though given the best education available as befitted his station. The learning of his time was at his disposal, and he excelled in his studies. He was married young, and already had a son when somehow, irked perhaps by the confinement within the palace, he persuaded his trusted charioteer to drive him into the town. On this fateful drive he encountered a sick man, an old man, a corpse, and an ascetic. Each time he had to ask his charioteer what they were, for he had never seen such things in his sheltered life. We must not think that he had never heard of these things, for his education must have acquainted him with their existence. However, there is all the difference in the world between knowing something in the abstract, and the sudden, living impact of confronting the thing itself.

It is a moot question whether Prince Gotama would have become the Buddha, had he been in living contact with those ineluctable facts of life from his earliest days; whether it was not just his sheltered life which drove him from the palace. *Dharma* is the immutable law, bringing about what is to become. *Karma* is its function; so, in spite of all human volitional attempts to achieve or to avoid, or perhaps just because of them, *Dharma* and *Karma* are and move with what is. This is one of the profound underlying fundamentals of Buddhism.

For Prince Gotama, the consequence of these fateful outings was the sudden discovery of what faces us all, compared with which his luxurious and pleasant life in the palace became as naught; he left it to find for himself the solution to his burning problem.

He took what was in his time the obvious step: he became a mendicant, and sought the best teacher, under whom he trained assiduously, both studying the teachings and practising austerities. His teacher offered him the succession as having no more to teach him. However, his own burning problem was not solved. He left and attached himself to another and equally renowned sage – to no avail; for though he was offered the succession again, his own problem was not yet solved.

So he decided to settle alone in the jungle, practising the utmost austerities, and thus finding a solution. This attracted some other mendicants, also seriously striving, who chose him as their teacher and settled with him. But although the recluse Gotama increased his practice of austerities, no solution appeared; and finally, emaciated and ill, he realised that he was near to death, without having found a solution.

It was at this point that Gotama, who became the Buddha, took another decisive step: he resolved to somehow arrive at an answer. He bathed himself in the river, cleansing his body, and accepted the offering of a bowl of milk to strengthen himself. Whereupon his followers left him on the grounds that he was no longer a true ascetic, but had taken to a soft life. However, he made himself a seat under a Bo-tree and vowed he would not get up from it until he had found the answer to his burning question.

Traditionally, at this stage Mara the Tempter appeared – the embodiment of the destructive principle – bent on dislodging the would-be Buddha. His guises are manifold, but the sequence is symbolically and psychologically important. For Mara first upbraided Gotama by bringing all the personal and cultural values into play, urging him to return, being duty bound as son and as heir to the throne; and also as a husband and father; accusing him of selfishly running away and shirking responsibility. But as Gotama paid no heed to him, Mara changed his tactics. He sent his daughters in their most alluring aspects to entice Gotama. He did not notice them. Then Mara, in a rage, changed them into a host of demons to assail Gotama who, holding steadfast to his purpose, sat unheedingly through this onslaught.

Tradition also beautifully describes how the would-be Buddha then sat for days wrapped in deep absorption and how things began to fall into place, until early one morning he looked up, saw the morning star and became the Awakened One, the Enlightened One, the Buddha.

The Way towards that realisation constitutes the body of his subsequent teachings. But his immediate reaction to that seeing was, 'Now I have seen you, builder of the house; the ridgepole is broken. Never will you build new houses again.' However, so tradition says, the Buddha also realised that what he had seen was not something that could be taught in words, nor did even the severest austerities result in it; he could conceive of no way to communicate to others what he had found and which constituted true deliverance.

This needed another insight, traditionally described as Brahma, the world spirit himself, intervening and suggesting that there were others seeking deliverance as sincerely and with as much dedication as he had, and that those whose 'eyes were but little covered with dust' would be able to grasp the message.

So the Buddha set out on his teaching career. He himself summed up the body of his teaching as, 'Suffering I teach, and the Way out of Suffering'. It became known as The Middle Way – not only as the balance between austerity and indulgence, but in a much deeper sense. Superficially, it is easily mistaken for turning one's back on suffering and walking away from it. But this is not what the Buddha did, nor can such a course bring succour. The Middle Way is seeing one's problems clearly, accepting and holding to them, and suffering them out; going right through the middle of them until one comes out the other end, where the eyes open and see. This is what the Buddha did.

This short account of the Buddha's Way mixes scriptures, tradition and legend. All stress the important stages and transitions which abstract description misses. If we are concerned with the Zen Way, we are well guided if we keep the Way of the Buddha in mind and ponder it in the heart, in depth. Outward conformity is empty imitation, to no purpose.

Right from the beginning, there is the young prince who, though brought up in sheltered luxury, is educated as befits his state and excels in the learning of his age, and who is also an expert in the kingly sports. The question already arises, how could such a one be confined within the limited walls and scope of any palace? Then, as a consequence of venturing forth, the sudden impact of actually meeting the verities of life face-to-face – which to him posed a personal problem of such magnitude that it made him leave the palace and seek an answer. Still following tradition, he went to the best teachers available, making his grade and proving his worth under them. What was available, he had incorporated and exhausted. Nowhere did he ever refuse it – that is important to keep in mind. He was not an irresponsible opter-out. But also, these efforts, however great, did not bring him the solution he sought. Therefore, still within the tradition, he increased his ascetic practices till they brought him to the point of death, with his problem still unanswered.

This seems to be a crucial stage. It does not come about without tremendous effort and very real achievement, which incidentally also brings some renown. But if the purpose holds and honesty perseveres, there takes place a stripping away of everything hitherto possessed or valued, to utter nakedness; and it seems that only in this state of true nakedness and poverty is an approach to real awakening possible – and safe.

Thus the Buddha at this stage found himself robbed of everything he was born to or had achieved by his own efforts. No longer a prince, heir and future ruler of a kingdom; no longer the outstanding disciple and would-be successor of two famous teachers; even left by his own few followers as an unworthy ascetic. He had nothing more to lose. Or to hold on to. With this nakedness he sat down under the Bo-tree.

When Mara, the tempter, appeared to swerve him from his purpose, how could a man, how could any I withstand that concerted onslaught. The weakling goes under, in the irresistible allure of that fascinating scale that slides down all the way from duty done, to greatness, to lust, and terror. This is why nakedness and absorption are so important; stripped of all outward trappings, and deeply absorbed, I is not there; and so no Mara can find sway, or get hold of what is not there. That is the message of this stage, and it is tremendous. But equally tremendous is that such deep absorption does not constitute awakening, it merely precedes it. Clarity comes afterwards, in the emerging from it. I has been lost, and with that a 'turning at the deepest seat of consciousness' has taken place, a true change of heart which has done with Mara, has sloughed off its wild and primitive energy which, transformed, now comes out as warmth of heart and clarity of seeing. This is seeing into the 'builder of the house' – I; and concern over how to communicate this to others, with near despair because of its utter incommunicability.

Hence nature itself, the world principle, takes a hand, and in the personification of Brahma exhorts the Awakened One to make the effort for the sake of fellow seekers who by their own endeavour have made themselves receptive, 'whose eyes are but little covered with dust'.

What did the Buddha see, and who is the builder of the house?

From his teaching, we can unravel that to some extent. What he 'saw' when he awoke from the dream or delusion which is that state of I, is things as they are; also that they are constantly changing – 'coming to be, and ceasing to be'. Hence the Middle Way of neither clinging to nor rejecting anything. With that everything becomes clear. Who, then, is the builder of the house?

A narrower view regards him as the builder of the house of flesh; thus release from the Wheel of Being, *Samsara,* by means of the ceasing of rebirth, which equals extinction, *Nirvana.* Such a narrow view is, however, not in accordance with the fundamentals of Buddhist teachings; a basic split between spirit and matter is foreign to Buddhism. One of the Three Signs of Being is Non-I; and what becomes extinct is not the rebirths of the house of flesh but the delusion of I. This latter is what constitutes awakening.

Buddhism regards spirit as inherent in, and not apart from, matter. The sequence is therefore not extinction but development, change, genuine transformation – and this is what is hinted at. It is also where the difficulty lies. As long as we are caught in the delusion of I, we cannot conceive of an I-less state; for to I, this is extinction.

Non-I, *Anatta,* is not an academic subject of discussion, but an immediate, vivid experience which rends the veil of delusion so that the eyes suddenly see clearly. The change occurs in the heart, its primitive emotionality being transformed. The latter constitutes the veil of delusion. Again, language helps us to understand such pictures, as the colours of emotions, like 'seeing red'.

We use language also euphemistically, as a kind of screen; or like a fence to keep out unwelcome trespassers. 'I have an emotion' is grammatically correct; but in fact it is the emotion that has me, and since I am thus possessed by it, I cannot lay down the emotion by an act of will.

Throughout the text, I is used in place of the more neutral term Ego. This choice decreases the abstraction of making Ego into something outside, into an object, whereas in fact it is perceived subjectively, intimately as I. As an exercise, the interested reader is asked to read this I in an entirely subjective sense, and to allow himself to become aware that one part of oneself is quite familiar with what is said about this subjective

I, and there is another part of one that would rather not be aware, is in the habit of turning its back to this awareness so as not to be obliged to see. The Zen Way seeks to transform these two components and then to merge them into a totality which comprises both, and so is whole.

At best, I can repress emotions, which is not wholesome, for thus rejected, the emotions become inaccessible and work up a head of steam underneath. Or the emotional energy discharges itself in fits of temper or moods; the more these are given into, the more frequent they become.

Emotional energy and its transformation will be discussed in the last two chapters. Neutrally, an emotion is an influx of energy which invades I and which approaches or exceeds the energy potential I can contain. Thus I am either carried away by it (see also p. 16, the quotation from Thomas Merton), or I try to somehow rid myself of the emotional upheaval. Both moves are unskilful, for they deal only with the manifestation of this energy, whereas the energy itself needs to be transformed. Before that can be undertaken, we need to remove the screens and fences we put up around ourselves, and dare really to look at our emotional reactions.

Take the short sentence: 'I want something'; a subject and an object, linked by the connecting verb. I see myself as other than and apart from what is Not-I which is capable of and often does interfere with my wants, needs, hopes and wishes. Accordingly, I feel myself in opposition to it, alienated from it, and threatened by it. This world which is other than I does not come up to my naive expectations of how it should be to suit me, my way, my ideas and ideals. Since I also know what is good and/or right both for me and the world, and indeed in my innermost core consider myself as the hub and centre of the world, the position of I is extremely precarious and vulnerable. I, mistakenly, seek to overcome this by possessing myself of the world so as to secure my position and allay my inherent insecurity. Whenever I am opposed and/or feel myself reduced, this evokes – at least emotionally if not consciously – my fear of extinction. Hence the violent, primitive emotional reaction when one of my dear wants or opinions or beliefs is threatened or thwarted. It is immaterial whether this reaction is total. Once it carried a survival value: on being threatened, instinctive energy arises and compels to action. The roots of it are indeed deep. Nor is this mechanism as such faulty, but when triggered off by the delusion of I, it operates in situations to which it does not belong; so we over-react, which causes us to act wrongly or blindly.

How did I become connected with this? 'I want something.' The clue lies in the 'want'. I am not consciousness as such, but am its reflecting function. As such, I is neutral, two-way as it were; 'I look at a flower – a flower looks at me'. In this, the object is known and of the same value as I, hence not other than I. It does not constitute a threat. Laurens van der Post[2] tells of the South African Bushmen that wherever they go, they feel themselves known, hence at home. There is no threat, no horror of emptiness or strangeness, only familiarity in a friendly, living environment, hence also the absence of any feeling of loneliness.

Habitual over-emphasis on I distorts this friendly mutual interaction, alienates I from 'other' into a separate, lonely and insecure bundle of arbitrary wishes and fears which feels

2. Laurens van der Post, *The Heart of the Hunter* (Penguin 1965), p. 188.

itself threatened by everything experienced as Not-I, other than I – particularly by what is 'totally other', what is outside the limited experience of I. This 'totally other' referred to here only in passing exerts the greatest fascination over I, forcing picture-making more than any other factor. However, I cannot conceive what is totally other; so all pictures are bound to be limited, faulty. This is expressed also in the Christian warning against 'graven images'.

I can be regarded as a lop-sided bundle, off-centre, insecure and under threat of losing my precarious balance. Naturally, I struggle towards some centre, but the centre that I can conceive of is born from the basic delusion. It is one of the many paradoxes that I have to face and work through, that the basic delusion both falsifies the image of the centre and compels the searching for it. This paradox is also the cause of I's constant effort to secure my position by increasing my powers and possessions. Since I cannot possess myself of the world, the delusion is obvious, the struggle hopeless, and the effort wrongly directed. Thus the very nature of I is brought into question, and with this we are at the core of the Buddhist quest. Thus also, the nature of I is shown to be seeking, usually perceived by I as wanting.

'I want something.' Yes, this 'want' is a deep, inherent urge, a drive of life-energy towards completion, towards conscious awareness of itself and towards manifestation/expression. This is the link-up, and even the picture-making compulsion makes sense. The tragedy and the promise of the human state are that I, being a small, distorted bundle, and exclusive of what is other than I, cannot conceive such totality, much less be aware of its living interrelation and interaction, whereas liberated from I there is a conscious living in this awareness and playing one's allotted part. Hence the Buddhist emphasis on the unreality of I; on the Way that leads from the delusions of I to the awakening of the totality of what is.

This life-energy is called, amongst other things, the Buddha Nature. And there is a saying in the Northern or Mahayana School of Buddhism that the Buddha Nature is the passions, and the passions are the Buddha Nature. It would be a mistake to interpret this on the surface meaning only. What is pointed at is the source, the energy itself.

Electricity as such is not perceptible, only its effects are. We use these as light, heat, and motor-power. Unharnessed, it discharges itself along zones of weakness and is destructive: lightning which strikes and kills or a broken power cable. We can transform electricity for domestic use in the home; but since it is a powerful ally, we install fuse boxes to ensure safety.

Primal energy, too, is perceptible only in its manifestations. In us human beings, the conscious I with its predilections comes in conflict with this energy which results in suffering for I. This suffering would effect the transformation if I could accept it. But if I reject the suffering, the energy remains blind but increases its potential. Sooner or later the conductor snaps. Or, more often, I am invaded by the energy but remain unaware of this take-over and appropriate the invading force as mine, thus unknowingly being carried away by it into a blind discharge of temper, or into equally blind fanaticism of intent, often mistaken as a 'strong personality'. A Chinese proverb expresses the danger of such a situation: 'He who bestrides the tiger may not dismount'.

Thus the passions and emotions are manifestations of that primal energy; its power, unless transformed and humanised, is unfit for domestic use. In the course of transformation, its blind or wild aspect changes, its awesome power is seen as such and understood as 'not mine', because not human. 'This mountain's summit is no place for human folk', as an old master expressed it.

This energy is, indeed, the essence and nature of all that is, of all that 'comes to be and ceases to be', of all striving and yearning, of growing and decaying; as that it is much more than human, and because of its demonic aspect has always been given the awesome attributes of divinity. In our irreligious days we have forgotten or ignore the awe of the impact of divinity, the God manifesting himself in the burning bush and laying down The Law, or as expressed in the apocryphal saying of Jesus 'who is near unto me, is near unto the fire'.

On 'this mountain's summit', it is experienced as such, and seen as my ground of being, as well as of all that is. But on the Zen Way, there is a further stage. There was the way up to 'this mountain's summit'; the full and conscious experience of this summit is essential, as well as the strength not to be swept away by its impact, of not losing one's humanity.

From that, there is the way down, that is by strictly keeping to one's human qualities (not being tempted!) to render this tremendous force in its human manifestations. The mystics of all ages have described these as threefold. As the light of seeing clearly what is, which is Wisdom; this is a total seeing, and exceeds the partial one which is the only seeing I am capable of with my mind and reason. As the warmth of the liberated heart, the Love which radiates of its own nature as the sun shines, and which is no longer bound to any objects or intentions. And as the strength or power which 'has gone beyond', utterly beyond my conceptions, and by virtue of which all are benefited.

Of such a man it is said that neither Buddha nor Mara can find him. He is not there, and the passions are transformed and humanised, are the Buddha Nature. He is and acts in harmony with it.

Mis-shunted by I with my predilections and choices, the energy either acts in blind eruptions, overwhelming me completely, or it rises along fissures, zones of weakness, compelling me to make a picture of it and to go out after the picture, thus forcing my co-operation; simpleton I is apt to take this energy as 'mine' or 'my will'.

It is important to be quite clear about this process. The nature of energy is movement, along gradients; coming to be, and ceasing to be, applies here too. Thus Life lives itself in and through its changing forms. If I am uncooperative, the potential rises to boiling point and the energy erupts blindly – hence its primitive character. The more uncooperative, the more deluded I am, the more primitive the energy, for it is forced to regress from ways of emergence that have already been forged but are now blocked by the faulty operation of I. This is why untrammelled emotionality makes man a brute, considerably below the level of an animal, which without an interfering I is naturally geared to respond correctly, and where the energy can therefore act as its compelling guide.

If I am not totally uncooperative, the energy, the urge, can only become conscious as wanting. Since I cannot consciously want without having an object that is wanted, I am forced to reflect that want as in a mirror which portrays or pictures that want. Becoming conscious of it, I, fired by the energy embodied in this 'want', can now go into action chasing that want to 'incorporate' it. And since this picture is a mirror image, it is related to I as such and constitutes what I miss for my completion – in my view. The delusion still holds sway. However, even this partial picture, because of its energy content, contains the fascination that the wanted object seemingly exercises over the subject, I. The tragedy is that I, deluded, have fashioned an inadequate picture, another limited object within the orbit of the known, for the unknown necessary for real completion is inconceivable to I. Thus I substitute an inferior object for what I really need for completion – a state in which I as I know myself, lose my sense of separateness and rejection, and in that merging am transformed. To I, this seems and is extinction – yet the yearning tends towards it. For in the extinction of I is my fulfilment, and with that the energy functions again out of its own nature; that is, the full warmth of the heart is released.

That is the importance of the human state. Only by becoming truly human is deliverance possible, and only then is conscious awareness of, and conscious cooperation with the life-energy, with the Buddha nature, possible. Delivered from the delusion of I with all its subsidiary delusions, the true human lives and acts in harmony with this nature. In the truly human heart forged by its own endeavour, this energy is reflected as warmth and clarity. Perhaps this is why from the side of I, deliverance, Nirvana, is described as cool – the opposite of the red hot passions and surging waves of fear. Seen from the other side, it is warm. A great contemporary Thai Buddhist teacher said to a Western disciple: 'When others come to us, we talk of suffering, and the Way that leads out of suffering; but among ourselves we talk of happiness and joy.'

However, we are not yet there. We are with the limited, inferior picture that I fashioned in order to be able to chase it, conquer it and possess it. Though fascination clings to all our wants, the more limited or modest the picture, the less the fascination, and the easier it is to obtain. A new hat or a new trendy article that catches my fancy is easily procured these days. But as soon as I obtain it, and the wish of my heart is – or seems to be – gratified, the fascination drops off the object; and after a period of restlessness and dissatisfaction, I am driven to fashion another picture which I can now pursue in full cry.

We all know this progression. Intellectually we can accept it, though the emotional acceptance is another matter and needs genuine transformation which is not easy, and with which the second part of this book will deal.

But there is still another angle to this object orientation. To recapitulate, in wanting something, I am compelled to make the wanting into a picture, which then is either confused with an object or draped over an object; thus I feel myself caught by the object, am deluded by the object – for it seems to me that it is the object that exerts the fascination and attraction rather than the 'I want', my own longing. An ideal example is the blinding fascination of attraction when we have fallen headlong in love. This love drapes itself like a shimmering, alluring veil over the object; perceptible to I is then only this magical attraction which is experienced as belonging to me – in a way rightly, for it is the self-portrait of the heart that has, as it were, jumped out in order to become visible so that I may become aware of what I really want. I, tragically, take it as belonging to the object. The latter need not be a person; we can also fall completely in love with an idea, with any -ism. And discover afterwards, when the veil is rent and the object becomes discernible, that it bears little if any relation to what I expected or thought it to be. Fortunately by that time the energy that comes with such a projection is all but spent. If not, the fascination of attraction turns into its opposite, love turns easily into hate, equally enthralling and binding. To the fascination of repulsion, too, clings an almost magical factor – as if God had turned devil. Not only our personal relationships swarm with such reversals, but they can also be observed in the history of religious movements and cults as an object lesson and very real warning.

Attraction and repulsion, affinity and neutrality, with their tremendous energy content, are what make and shape this world, from atoms to planets. We are of the same stuff. The doctrine of Non-I points out this impersonal aspect. Usually, I confronting 'other than I' react and am apt to be carried away by the energy which I mistake for my own and which I experience as attraction or repulsion. Neutrally, seen with the 'single eye', there is only compatibility or incompatibility; seen as such, there is no emotional reaction. Thus unbound from the shackles of delusion, action is free, spontaneous, and in harmony with the situation. This is 'right action'. It is also human action; in our world the lion does not lie down with the lamb; and we are human beings, neither gods nor demons, nor supermen.

Concretely, the power of repulsion is just as total as that of attraction, and just as gripping. But in our everyday life we can learn not to allow ourselves to be carried away into action by it. For the harder we try to reject and repulse, the more power we give to the object which we reject; this applies whether the rejected picture seems to be outside or inside.

The more I push against a table, the more the table seems to push against me. A little child, having run into a corner of the table, will slap the table, 'naughty table'. We laugh, but do not know we act likewise, though not quite so obviously.

As a girl, I learned to ride a bicycle on a rough but very wide country road. Wobbling along insecurely, knowing it was still difficult for me to dismount, I dreaded the occasional larger stone on the road. Bracing myself to avoid it, fighting it, fully intent not to be unsaddled by it, I hit it head-on every time, with plenty of room to pass either side! Later on, I found it quite difficult to hit such a stone intentionally. One can learn from these things.

But if the object is irrelevant, we are now left with the truncated sentence of 'I want', though I know not what, but with the characteristic dissatisfaction and restlessness resulting from the emotional energy as it begins to work up pressure. If the energy does not escape outward into a picture and the subsequent release of chasing it, it turns inward and attacks what is still there: I.

This is a dangerous stage, and hence we have all the training analogies of forging, shaping, changing. Here it will suffice to say that the rigid structure of an I which holds down the natural outflow of energy is likely to get shattered as and when the repressed energy reaches explosion point. Hence the need for training which softens that structure, makes I malleable as it were by interaction with that energy. This is a two-way process of participation. Both sides take part in it and become changed by it, thus approaching each other, and in so doing merging into one whole, a totality that is utterly different. The two constituents themselves must have changed before the merging can take place, before they are 'mergeable'.

Now we can look again at our truncated sentence, 'I want'. I is lost in the process, or so it seems, because I have changed; and the want itself is also changed, in fact constitutes just what I really want but can never see. I can only become it by ceasing to be I!

This ceasing is the fulfilment of the want, the fulfilment of the heart. The eyes are open and see clearly, the heart is open, freed from all alienation, insecurity and fear, thus radiating warmth. Light and warmth, these are the two aspects of the liberated, humanised energy.

Hence the Buddha is both the All-Enlightened One with the 'single eye' of Wisdom, and the All-Compassionate One with a heart that radiates Love. That is why it is said that his very body was the colour of gold – the liberated warmth of the heart shines and flows of itself, is perceptible and touches the heart of the beholder, warms and encourages him, and inclines him to become likewise.

This is the message of the Buddha. In its grandest conception it points forward into the future, towards what is not yet known or understood. Perhaps the deepest aspect of *Ahimsa,* harmlessness, is that it equals non-interference. One of the great sages of our time, Ramana Maharshi, when asked how a liberated person helps others, replied: 'When you have become the Self (Non-I), there are no others.' A wise Rabbi, when asked by an outstanding student: 'In the olden days there were men who could see the face of God. Why can nobody see it today?' answered: 'My son, because nowadays nobody can stoop so low.'

In the Zen school of Buddhism it is said that the liberated man leaves no trace; that neither Buddha nor Mara can find him. We are reminded of Gotama sitting in meditation under the Bo-tree when Mara, the tempter, assailed him in vain. And of Brahma himself asking the Awakened, the Buddha, to make available what he had seen to those 'whose eyes are but little covered with dust'.

There is true readiness and true receptivity for heart touching heart. The late Master Sesso once said that the liberated heart is so full of warmth that it needs must flow out, and in so doing touches every heart it comes in contact with, and incites it to become likewise.

So the true spreading of the teaching of the Buddha is in liberating one's own heart, rather than in the preaching of doctrines. There is a tacit injunction to talk of the teaching only when invited, which presupposes the readiness of asker (see above, Brahma asking the Awakened). It is not a matter of trying to persuade others and thus consciously interfering. The latter is *karma-producing* action. Of the liberated man it is said that he leaves no trace; he has sloughed off I with its conscious intentions and its itch to interfere.

If *Dharma* is the immutable law inherent in what is, then *Karma* is its function. Derived from the Sanskrit root *'Kar'*, it means act, deed, and constitutes the link between cause and effect. As that, it is the normal cycle of nature, of 'coming to be and ceasing to be', in the impermanence of all things through which Life lives itself and develops.

A further connotation is added in the human realm, where *karma-producing* actions are conscious, volitional, intentional acts and deeds instituted by I, and which shape personal fate and character from past to present and into the future.

Since in Buddhism these acts comprise thought, word and deed, the character-shaping component is obvious. Doctrinally, consistently good action will wear out bad *Karma* accumulated in this or former lives, and thus will merit future rebirths in happier states of existence, either in comfortable human situations or among the heavenly beings. However, those states are themselves impermanent, and are still existence on the Wheel of Being, not deliverance from it which may be achieved only by actively following a path of training which leads to the shedding of I.

In the I-less or awakened state, I-intentional actions have ceased as there is no I to instigate them. Thus the liberated man has sprung himself out of existence on the Wheel, out of *Karma,* leaves no trace, and is no longer a '*karma-producing being*'.

In the picturesque language of religion, and as a hope for a future to come, the true attainment of the human state is fore-shadowed, intuited as it were. Today when violence has become almost a commonplace, it holds out a special promise: the wildness that clings to I can be worked out, the rapaciousness and violence that seems our lot through the ages can be ended.

For when I lose the blinkers of delusion and with that my fear, I also lose the perennial itch to interfere and to manipulate others. And with that the state is reached again where reciprocally man looks at man, feels himself known, thus finds the other fair.

The treading of that Way is possible only by oneself, no one can do it for one. This restores dignity to the individual who is almost reduced to a cypher today. It is a responsible way of truly delivering oneself from the trammels and blinkers of compelling delusions and so to be free of I-notions; simply by being, *wu-wei* (non-interference), the inherent warmth of the heart flows naturally, encouraging and inciting others to do likewise of their own free will; to enter the Way from their own heart's desire, and to walk it to their own heart's fulfilment, thus proclaiming the Way.

This is the Way of the Buddha, wide as the world, and open to all who are minded to tread it, following his footsteps, in gratitude. It may be trodden now no less than in the past. And the message of the Buddha is as appropriate today as it ever was. It points the Way – but leaves it to us to heed it. Within the scheme of things, we ourselves are the makers of our fate.

HISTORICAL DEVELOPMENT

The teaching of the Buddha, as it has come down to us, is reflected or refracted in various schools. This development is important for a survey of so vast a subject matter, but is not within the scope of this book. There are excellent and detailed accounts of it, both traditional and in the light of modern scholarship, that incorporate, at least in part, material which has only recently come to light. (See Further Reading, p. 149.)

However diversified the various Buddhist schools and teaching lines seem, all rest soundly on the basic principles.

Here it suffices to say that in time there developed two major traditions, one being that of the Southern School or Way of the Elders with Pali as the scriptural language. This school, still extant in South-East Asia, is the sole survivor of various other schools now long extinct. It is found predominantly in Ceylon, Burma and Thailand. In India, the homeland of the Buddha, a resurgence of Hinduism and the Moslem invasion displaced Buddhism. The Northern tradition, based originally on Sanskrit as the scriptural language, but then translated into the languages of the host countries, is found today mainly in Japan and Korea. In China and Tibet, where most of its lines were formalised and developed, it has been expelled.

The Zen School is a line of this Northern tradition. 'Zen', derived from the Sanskrit *Dhyana,* through the Chinese transliteration *Ch'an,* literally means meditation. Thus the Zen School of Buddhism is a meditative school of Buddhism; however, we shall see that meditation is not its only practice. There are accounts of its historical inception in China, its development there, the flowering during the T'ang dynasty, its re-emergence after the various persecutions of Buddhism in China, its introduction to Japan at the beginning of the 13th century where it survives in the forms of the Rinzai and Soto Zen Schools. The long, slow decline of all Buddhism in China after the Sung dynasty, partly because of the arising of the native Neo-Confucianism, and partly because of more persecutions from which the Ch'an School emerged as the most vigorous so that all surviving Buddhist lines combined under its name. Known in Japan as Ming Zen, this line was introduced there in the 17th century and still continues.

Soon after its beginning in China, the Zen School developed teaching lines in continuity with the styles of great masters who subsequently were considered to be the founders. Two of those, Rinzai and Soto Zen, were introduced to Japan in this way to be there further developed and adapted in harmony with the Japanese mentality.

In the Rinzai Zen line, a major reform took place in Japan after Master Hakuin at the beginning of the 19th century. Today in Japan the Zen School consists of three traditional lines: the Rinzai and Soto Zen Schools, which are both Sung Zen, and the Obaku School or Ming Zen, which incorporates other Buddhist traditions, specifically Pure Land.

Historically, the birthplace of Zen is China where the developed Buddhism of India was modulated by the practical and concrete mentality of the Chinese, and in time took on features in harmony with the native culture, incorporating as always some of the basic assumptions of the host country.

There is justification for saying that the Zen School constitutes a return from the profound but highly intricate philosophical and psychological systems of the Northern School to the basic Buddhist teachings. This return was facilitated by one of the native Chinese systems, that of Taoism, which at its best likewise advocates simplicity and accord with what is. Indeed, '*Tao*' literally means 'the Way' of living in such accord and harmony. This 'Way', and its corollary, '*wu-wei*' or non-interference, was readily adopted by the Zen School.

Traditionally, it is said that the Indian monk Bodhidharma brought the Zen School to China, and became its first Chinese patriarch, but that it was only after Eno, the sixth Chinese patriarch, that the Zen school became specifically Chinese. Actually it was only in the generation after Eno (Hui Neng) that the School grew and developed its characteristic features. Though neither Bodhidharma nor Eno are historically documented, the tradition that grew around them points out the fundamental attitudes of the Zen School, and as a living tradition, this is more important for the practitioner than historical facts.

Soon after its emergence the Zen School, partly by predilection and partly for training purposes, moved its monasteries into remote regions where the monks' livelihood was only possible by engaging in physical work, farming the land – a practice unknown to the Indian Sangha or community of monks. For the Zen School, labour itself became one of its important training devices. 'A day without work is a day without food.'

TRAINING IN A JAPANESE ZEN MONASTERY

To enter a Zen training monastery is not possible without relevant pre-training. What causes a young man to take up this career nowadays?

He may meet a Zen priest who impresses him, or he may have been in some emotional trouble and have gone for advice to a Zen priest of whom he may have heard, or he may simply find himself in need of more 'strength' than he can muster; but whatever the reason, his first step is to become acquainted with the priest of a particular Zen temple. He may go there repeatedly, and if he finds it answers his needs, he will go more frequently, and take part in the temple's activities and daily work, spend an occasional weekend there, and, should he wish, receive permission to live in for a time. If he fits into the life and likes it, he may stay and ask to be ordained as a novice. If the temple priest considers him suitable, he will accept him, thus becoming his Dharma Father, with full rights and responsibility over him.

The life of a novice is not easy. Perhaps the best comparison is that of an apprentice in a medieval craft. As yet, he is not considered capable of doing anything, and so is the unpaid slave of the household and is kept busy at all the menial tasks without a moment to himself. He cannot do what suits him, and so learns little by little the all-important lesson of giving in easily, of placing his I in a secondary position. He has to fit in smoothly. Indeed, if he cannot do so, he will leave, and will be encouraged to do so.

His noviciate is the starting point for entry into a training monastery; he could not settle into that without this softening-up process, his pre-training as a novice.

As a novice, he learns to work in the house, the temple and the garden, cleaning, cooking and pruning. A certain behaviour or deportment is expected of him. He also learns to look after the priest, to serve him and to be there for him. He learns to clean religious implements and images, often precious, to polish lacquer work, to whisk and serve the thick ceremonial tea, to take care of the robes, both the everyday and the special ones, washing, folding, repairing and storing them. He also learns the usual Sutras and the chanting of them and the daily and seasonal religious observances that are held in the temple.

His day starts fairly early, at about 5 a.m. The first activity on rising is the Sutra chanting in the Hondo or shrine room. That is usually followed by breakfast, and afterwards cleaning, wet-mopping the wooden gangways which surround every temple or traditional Japanese house, sweeping, and then doing the outdoor work, in front of the temple gate, in the garden, in the cemetery, or whatever cleaning there is to be done.

If the novice happens to go to school or college, he will leave in time to attend. As soon as he returns home, he goes on with his chores until the evening meal is over. Having cleared up, he may then use the evening for his studies; at 9 p.m. there is another Sutra chanting. His weekends and vacations are filled with the same work. He also helps at the special ceremonies that take place in the temple, and so gets used to the routine of temple life.

His Dharma Father assumes complete authority over him and since he has no time to himself, that strong I which likes to do things 'as it suits me', gets slowly gentled and smoothed. He has to learn to handle his emotional reactions while functioning correctly in the temple routine.

A temple is rather like a church. There are the ceremonies of the religious year with their particular rites and observances. The eighth of April is the Buddha's birthday; the 15th of February is his death anniversary; and the eighth of December is the commemoration of his enlightenment. There is also the memorial day, which is the death anniversary of the founder of that particular temple. Other important occasions in the yearly calendar are the autumn and spring equinoxes which are usually connected with services for the dead. Next to New Year, mid-August is the busiest time in a temple, it is O Bon, a kind of All Souls: cemeteries are put in order, Sutras are read for the dead, and many visitors are received. It lasts for about a week including the preparations.

The main festive commemoration is the inauguration of the New Year, which is also a period of great activity and lasts for about two weeks. Preparations start a couple of days before. The 31st of December sees a thorough 'spring cleaning'; all the woodwork and ceilings are dusted and wiped, all the furniture is moved out and washed and even the floor mats are taken out with their frames and beaten; and all the cupboards, shelves, crockery and kitchen utensils are washed. By the time everything is spick and span, it is usually late into the night. The fires are extinguished and new ones lit in the New Year; the first bath of the New Year is taken, new clothes are ready for the morning service, and after breakfast New Year visitors begin to arrive. Traditional New Year's food is prepared in advance so there is hardly any cooking to be done, but as all the visitors are formally received and served with ceremonial tea, and conducted out, it is a busy time, though it is also a relaxed and joyful time after the hectic activities of the preceding days.

The novice gets used to all these activities and learns to take his part in them. And after a number of years, if he decides that this is really his vocation, his Dharma Father may consider the novice ready to enter a training monastery to become a monk.

A temple serves its parishioners. As an ordained temple priest, the incumbent is responsible for the activities of his temple. There is the pastoral care of his parishioners who come and see him. There is a certain amount of social activity involved; and there are all the seasonal ceremonies as well as the funeral rites and services.

In the past – though no longer – a temple also functioned as a school where children or adults could learn to read and write. The late Master Sesso once explained that the white sand that is so often found in front of shrine rooms helped to brighten them as they served also as teaching rooms.

Temples, like traditional Japanese houses, are fairly open; wooden posts keep up the structure and support the ceiling. Removable sliding doors, and wood frames papered over with translucent rice paper, act as walls and partitions. As the fire hazard in such structures is great, any form of heating is discouraged.

The incumbent of a temple has to be an ordained priest, and as such he is different from a monk. However, he needs to have been a monk to be eligible for ordination. Since the Meiji restoration (1896) an ordained priest may marry.

A training monastery is different from a temple and its activities. Usually translated as 'monastery', it is not one in the usual sense of the word. The monk does not spend his whole life in it. It is more appropriately thought of as a training seminary, and after being ordained as priest the monk eventually leaves it to take over a temple. In the Zen line, which is what we are concerned with here, particularly the Rinzai line, only the Roshi or Master of such a monastery is a monk in our sense of the word, because once he has moved in as the Master, he remains there for good.

The period that a monk spends in the monastery varies greatly depending on whether he is to take over, or wishes to take over, a little country temple where his responsibilities are small and not too many demands are made on him, or a big temple, or a temple with traditional training facilities for lay people, where he has to have a much longer training period in the monastery. Once ordained, it is for the priest to decide whether he wishes to encourage his parishioners to come for occasional communal services, to what extent he takes part in the life of his community and the amount of pastoral care that he offers. Certain of his duties are fixed, however, such as daily morning and evening services, seasonal ceremonies, and all funeral rites. He may take in and teach novices, give talks to and hold meditation sessions for the laity.

When the novice has undertaken to seek admission into a training monastery, his Dharma Father then makes arrangements for him to enter a specific monastery. The entrance into a training monastery constitutes an extremely hard test. Should the young man decide, as a novice, that this is not really his vocation, he is free to leave with thanks to his Dharma Father. But once he has entered the monastery it is not so easy for him to leave, although he is free to do so. A slight social stigma adheres to a fully ordained monk who abandons the monastery – perhaps because society considers that he is not reliable.

The extremely severe test of one week's 'entrance begging' helps the young man to find out how serious his intentions are. The monastery is advised that the young man is due to come. The usual time to enter is spring, any time from mid-March, but it is considered that all new applicants should have arrived before 8 April, the Buddha's birthday.

On leaving the temple, the postulant receives from his Dharma Father a new set of robes and all that he needs for the monastery. Traditionally he carries a bundle of his belongings and a box which contains his credentials, a certificate that he is a novice and entitled to beg for his food on his way to the monastery, and also a slip or envelope containing money to pay for his funeral should he die on the way. Though nowadays he is allowed to use public transport, and his Dharma Father pays for his ticket, he must arrive on foot at the monastery.

He passes through the big gate, through the front garden, and steps into the entrance hall.

In traditional Japanese-style houses, this is usually paved and has steps leading into the house proper. In the past, somebody always had to be at home, for though the house could be barred from inside, it could not be locked from outside. A visitor steps into the entrance hall and draws attention by calling out, then waits until somebody appears. On being invited up, he discards his footwear on the steps; shoes are not worn inside. Temples and monasteries follow this traditional pattern.

So, standing in the entrance hall, the novice calls out. The head monk, who acts also as guest master, comes to see who has arrived. The novice asks for permission to enter the monastery.

Invariably he is told it is full, that there is no room, that the life is too hard and not for him, and to go away. The postulant refuses to do this, and presents his credentials. These are looked over, checked through, and he is again told to go away. He refuses a second time, and possibly a third time, upon which the head monk leaves. The postulant, determined to stay, remains in the entrance hall. He takes off his bundle, places it on the low bench and settles himself in a crouching position over it. To sit sideways, crouched over a bundle, however fully packed, with the head down on the hands folded on the bundle in a supplicating position, is not easy to endure. He is given food, and for the night he is allowed to come in and sleep, but the nights are short in a monastery. He has to remain there for three days, but two or three times a day he will be told to leave. He refuses and is then grabbed and forcefully thrown out; he is dragged all the way from the entrance hall through the garden to the main gate which is then guarded so that he cannot come back for at least half an hour. It is very harsh treatment, and upon arrival the young postulants know that they are in for a real ordeal.

Having personally seen this happen year after year, I once asked the head monk whether it was necessary to be so frightfully severe with the young postulants who were blue in the face from exhaustion, fear and anticipation of further trials. I asked whether they had to be manhandled and thrown out in this way on top of being frightened and in pain from their crouching. The head monk nodded and explained: 'Yes; but it serves a dual purpose. Seen from their side, it is the hardness of the test, the fear of the unexpected that comes with it, and the awe. It is necessary for them; we always tell them, "If you really want to come in, you must leave your self outside, and then you will have no difficulty in the training. But if you take your self inside, you will have nothing but difficulties yourself, and make difficulties for the community." It is for the gentling of this self (the I), to help them to drop it and leave it outside, that the treatment is and must be harsh. But it serves another and very important purpose as well, though this the postulant does not know. To keep crouching for three days is almost impossible; we know it from our own experience. So we chase the postulant out, throwing him to the ground a couple of times, and while manhandling him, we see that his muscles get a bit loosened up. Then we guard the gate so that he has a chance to sit in an upright position for a while. When he has recovered a little, we let him in again, and he has to go on with his crouching. Young, weak, puny ones, who haven't got much strength, we throw out three or four times a day. With the sturdier ones, it is necessary only twice. It is hard work for us, too, but without it, nobody could endure the strain.'

It is from things like this that one sees how the living practice, the living experience, works both ways. There is all the harshness to test whether the postulant's discipline so far has given him sufficient strength – not only to stick it out, but more important, to still keep his form. Master Hakuin's words come to mind: 'To bear what is unbearable, and to endure what is unendurable.' Such holding out can reduce one to a howling bundle of conflicting emotions; real, religious discipline shaped over years transforms this into the strength to keep both one's head and one's form under all circumstances – a positive strength without which further training or development cannot take place. As Master Rinzai said, 'The old masters had ways of making men'. Where this is still a living tradition, there is also the other side, an understanding of such crucial tests or transition periods, and though covertly, the necessary help and support are given.

After the postulant has endured those three days in the entrance he is allowed into the actual building on the fourth day and is brought to a small annexe of the shrine room where, with his bundle, he has to sit facing the wall and an incense burner for another three days. Again, he gets his food and is allowed to sleep at night, but otherwise remains in this position, not even relieved by occasionally being thrown out. Three sides of this annexe are open to wind and weather, and also to anybody who happens to pass, or comes to see how he is doing. If he begins to itch or move ever so slightly, he is pounced upon. Thus another three days pass.

Some postulants give up, and are not blamed for it, but surprisingly those are few and far between.

In the evening of the sixth day the postulant is called before the head monk, who again admonishes him to leave his self outside, and to work hard. He is then led into the meditation hall which also serves as the dormitory. There he makes his prostrations to Manjusri, enshrined in every meditation hall, the Bodhisattva who with his sword of wisdom cuts the bonds of ignorance. The Keisaku, the flat, sword-like stick, is a symbol of this sword that helps us in our training. The new monk is then allotted his place in the hall to sit and to sleep.

With this, he has been received into the community of monks, and is now a first-year monk. This means that he is at the beck and call of everybody, even another first-year monk who happened to have been received only a day earlier. He owes complete obedience to his superiors and elders. Of the first-year monk it is said that he may not show his teeth or smile; all he is expected to say when spoken to is 'yes', and that with a lowered head.

As a first-year monk, he starts Sanzen, the koan interviews from the Master. Koans, literally 'public documents', are recorded cases of questions or phrases which had proved helpful for a trainee to awaken. They are used for that purpose in the Rinzai School of Zen Buddhism. Traditionally, it is said they serve as door-knockers – to open the gateless gate.[3]

The new monk also learns more Sutras, the beating rhythms of the wooden sounding board, the drum, the clappers and the Wooden Fish. The last, a hollow wooden drum in the shape of a foreshortened carp, of various sizes, is used for chanting, its beats indicating speed and rhythm. He also learns the leading of the dedications for the Sutra chanting.

This learning, like all learning in Zen training, has a strong physical component, and goes according to the proverb: 'Better than learning it, get used to it.' Instead of filling one's head with 'how to ... ' and becoming muddled by the complications, just try ... and try ... and try until it comes. So that whenever the young monk is put on any new task – those change every six months – he is given basic instructions, and then expected to manage by himself. He may practise in his free time, and ask an elder brother to supervise and correct him. His first 'public appearance' usually coincides with the opening ceremony of a retreat. Should he fail to come up to average standard, the head monk and even the Master may yell a correction. It says much for

3. See Miura and Sasaki, *Zen Dust.* First Zen Institute of America.

the strength of keeping the form and for the long discipline of obedience, that I have never seen a monk flustered into further mistakes by such fierce correction in public.

But above all, the young monk has to adapt himself to the yearly routine of life in the monastery. This attitude of adapting oneself easily and smoothly to varying circumstances is much encouraged. Little is taught overtly; the new monk is expected to keep his eyes skinned, to pick up how things are done quickly and eagerly, and to keep them in mind. He is judged by his ability to do so; rightly, for 'my way' is the way of I, and that needs to be sloughed off.

Monastic life is a regulated life. The day starts with the duty monk going round the sleeping quarters at a brisk trot, with his morning cry and bell awakening the sleepers. These get up at once and roll up their sleeping-quilts. The big bell that hangs in a little tower over the entrance gate to the compound begins to boom in a slow rhythm for about 15 minutes, the time for the morning toilet. This consists of getting dressed and running into the forecourt where around a circular trough cold water is dashed over the face, and the mouth rinsed, using wooden ladles to scoop up the water.

Then the monks file into the shrine room for the Sutra chanting. A covered flagstone path leads from the monks' quarters to the shrine room. In common with Japanese tradition, footwear is essential out of doors, but is discarded when stepping into the house, or generally indoors. Monks wear the traditional straw sandals with thongs on bare feet. These are common property; they are carefully lined up when stepping out of them backwards up the entrance step, so that they face outwards. On leaving, one steps into them and walks away.

The Zendo head monk leads the procession of monks carrying a little gong mounted on a handle. With it, all necessary signals are given for entering, bowing and sitting down on the bare tatami mats that constitute the floor in temples and traditional Japanese houses. The big gong is struck and the chanting begins. The Master also comes from his quarters to take part.

Afterwards the monks are led back into the meditation hall where they do a short chanting while a duty monk goes round chanting individually before every little shrine in the monastery, especially in the kitchen, bath, toilets, and the entrance hall. After that, Zazen (sitting Zen) starts, and soon the Sanzen bell rings and the monks file out once more to take their place kneeling in the Sanzen row behind the Sanzen bell, awaiting their turn for an interview with the Master.

On hearing the monk before him strike the bell and leave for his interview, the monk bows, stands up, bows deeply and goes forward to take his place at the bell, waiting for the Master's handbell in the Sanzen room to sound the end of the present interview. Then he strikes the bell twice, gets up, bows, and goes to the interview room.

Traditional Rinzai Zen interviews are short, and may be quite fierce. However, great formality is observed on entering and leaving, prostrating oneself both at the threshold and in front of the Master. The interview over, the monk returns to the meditation hall. As soon as the signals for the end of the interviews are sounded, the breakfast bell rings and all file into the refectory for the morning meal. When first daylight comes either during the interviews or during breakfast the wooden block is sounded in its special rhythm. The time for striking it is in the morning when indoors one can see the lines in the palm of one's hand and in the evening when one can no longer see them.

After breakfast there is first of all the sweeping outside the monastery gate, then the inside sweeping and wet-mopping of all the wooden floors and the gangways that surround and connect the shrine room, the Master's quarters, the main buildings, and the meditation hall with its annexes.

The day is spent working in the gardens and the grounds. The midday meal is before 12 a.m. Usually there is almost an hour's break afterwards – to be used for study, looking up texts, or for rest. Then more work until the 'medicinal meal' around 5 p.m. in summer. This is eaten without chanting, and consists of leftover rice from the midday meal, hot tea and pickles, perhaps also leftover soup which is warmed up.

The Indian Sangha or community of monks had two meals a day, and nothing was eaten after midday. These rules still apply, but in a cold country like Japan in winter, and as indeed first instituted in the early Zen monasteries in China which arose in isolated places and had to be self-supporting for their food, physical work became the rule for monks as distinct from the southern Sangha who only beg for food. The Hyakujo Rules, laid down for the early Chinese Zen communities by Master Hyakujo, are still followed by Zen monasteries in Japan. His motto was 'a day without work is a day without food', and he himself lived up to this. When his monks hid his working tools to prevent the old and weak master from exhausting himself, he simply refused to eat; his tools were returned. So, though colder climate and hard physical work made an evening snack desirable for health and strength, it is regarded as medical treatment rather than food. Therefore there is no chanting, and it is got over quickly.

The morning and midday meals are considered forms of meditation and recollection. The Zendo head monk leads the monks into the refectory. They line up, the nest of eating bowls which they bring with them in their hands. The head monk signals with the clappers, all bow and sit down. The chanting begins, during which the meal is served. A further signal, and the meal is eaten in silence. Strict formality is observed throughout. Afterwards, tea or just hot water is served, which is also used to swill the bowls, while the thanksgivings are chanted. The bowls are then wiped with the cloth that is kept with them and tied up once more in their wrappers. Then the end of the meal signal is given and all stand up, bow again, and are led back into the meditation hall.

Though the same silence is observed during the 'medicinal meal', there is no chanting. After that there is Zazen, with Sanzen, till bed-time at 10 p.m. An evening off is rare.

Such is the life the new monk leads when he has been accepted into the community. The time is usually the end of March or beginning of April. Though new postulants may join either the Summer Retreat or the Winter Retreat, the Summer one is the easier in terms of weather and sitting hours. Hence it is the custom to arrive in time for this one.

Once the new monk is settled in, his life becomes routine, but as yet he knows little of the interruptions to this routine; that is, the seasonal changes of the monastic year.

Mid-April usually brings a week's begging tour into a country area. This may be quite strenuous as the monks have to go out in all weathers, often in snow; shod only in straw sandals, their feet get chafed, and they have to cart along the increasingly heavy loads of begged rice. They put up in temples for the night.

The end of April is the first little Sesshin which heralds the beginning of the Summer Retreat on 1 May, and the Great Sesshin which starts it. 'Sesshin' means something like recollection of the heart, and is a time of increased meditation during which other work is stopped. Little Sesshins last for five days, with a certain amount of work. Great Sesshins last for seven days, and none except the essential work is done. There are seven such Great Sesshins in the year, three during the Summer Retreat, and four during the Winter Retreat.

The evening before the Great Sesshin, the monks have ceremonial tea with the Master. The opening ceremony for the Summer Retreat starts with a special Teisho which is later than the usual time of 8 a.m. Teisho is the Master's reading of and commenting on one of the Koan texts. It normally takes place two or three times a week, and is given during Retreat periods only, which amounts to seven months in the year. It takes about one year to get through the *Mumonkan*.[4]

Teisho is announced first by the big bell over the gate which is struck at intervals as in the early morning. This is then taken up by the sounding of the wooden block with a special rhythm as at daybreak and dusk. The last beat of this is the signal for the big drum outside the shrine room to be struck. The drum-beats gradually work up into a tattoo during which the monks are led into the shrine room and take their places. With the final crescendo the Master arrives, conducted by the head monk carrying the text book carefully wrapped in a brocade folder.

4. Zenkei Shibayama, *Zen Comments on the Mumonkan* (Harper & Row 1974).

Other priests and some specially connected lay people also come to the opening Teisho. The shrine room is decorated with the festive candlesticks, incense burners, flower vases and brocade hangings. Otherwise it follows the usual Teisho pattern.

The Master approaches and enters the shrine room as the drumming reaches a crescendo, which stops sharply as he bows. At that, the big gong is struck and the Sutra chanting begins. The Master takes part in it, indeed one could say he demonstrates the spirit of it, bowing, spreading his prostration mat before the altar, prostrating himself, getting up and going forward to put incense on the brazier, then back to the mat and more prostrations, and towards the end of the chanting he ascends the traditional High Seat. The reading stand is put in front of him with the text open for him to start reading. This he does as soon as the chanting ends, reading a short passage only. He is then handed a bowl of thick ceremonial tea which he drinks, and then comments on the text. Whatever he says and does is 'pointing' for his students.

For the opening Teisho, the Sutra chanting is longer, and after the Master descends from the High Seat, he prostrates himself again; all heads are down on the ground in prostration, and the Retreat is declared open.

This is followed by a meal for all who attended. By 1 pm it is all cleared away, and the Sesshin continues. Sleeping hours are curtailed: 11 p.m. to 3 a.m. and most of the time is spent in sitting meditation, Zazen. 'Collecting the heart' means bringing it back from the outside where it disports itself, and learning to stay at home or finding one's home from which one can then sally forth but come back to again, no longer losing the way home; no longer a displaced person, driven about by circumstances beyond one's control.

During Great Sesshins with the long meditation hours, there are usually three Sanzen interview periods a day, early morning, afternoon and evening.

It is a time of concentrated effort. The new monk is under pressure from two sides, from the Zendo head monk who sees that his sitting is correct and attentive, and from the Master who demands his insight into the Koan he has been given. As the Sesshin continues and the long sitting hours begin to tell, a further device is used: on leaving the interview room to return to the meditation hall, the new monk is intercepted by the Zendo head monk who bars his way and tells him to join the Sanzen queue once more for another interview. Thus squeezed, he may and indeed is often intended to try to fight his way back into the meditation hall; quite lively scenes may develop. These, too, serve a purpose, for the sudden flare-up may help the monk out of an impasse. It is always short and within understood limits.

But even a Great Sesshin comes to an end, and the monk begins to settle in; for the time being he has come through the hardest tests, the 'entrance begging', and a Great Sesshin. Now he has only to contend with the routine of a very hard life; rising at 3 a.m., manual work, complete obedience, careful deportment, no time to himself, and, of course, his reactions to this life, and to his elder brothers. He works, eats, sleeps, sits with them. He is bound to find something or somebody irksome and difficult.

His closest companions are the other first-year monks, and it is really only with these that he can talk and also air his feelings. At the beginning of June the monks change into summer robes. Mid-June, the middle of the Summer Retreat, is the second Great Sesshin. It is more unpleasant than the May one because it falls in the rainy season and the mosquitoes swarm in the sultry heat.

Work gets rather hard, too; weeds sprout under those conditions, and the gardens need much attention. There is no relief from the clammy heat, and the strain begins to tell.

This is the time when that blessed hour after the midday meal sees the new monks huddled in a corner of the gardens, out of sight, talking with each other, airing their grievances, realising they are in the same boat, telling stories of encouragement, and the odd joke which makes their lot easier to bear. This, though unknown to the new monks, is a considered device to help them settle in.

I remember a year when there was only one new monk. To his face, everybody was as gruff as usual, but behind his back conferences were held about what to do and how to help him as he had nobody to let himself go with, and thus get some relief. So daily he would find an apple or some fruit or dainty smuggled under his sitting cushion; accidentally the serving monk happened to fish out the tastiest morsel when ladling food into his bowl; some little daily gratification to help him – and it did the trick. He turned out a very fine monk, and a good priest later.

Being together through all the difficulties forges a very strong bond between monks of the same year. However far they may be separated after leaving the monastery, there will be occasional visits, and always New Year greetings for the rest of their lives.

The 15th of July is the day when the monastery celebrates O Bon. For the two weeks preceding that, the monks spend every free minute and part of their short night hours making all kinds and shapes of paper lanterns, often beautifully painted and inscribed. On that day, the meditation hall is decorated; every monk sets up on his place a little family altar with ancestor tablets, an offering, and all the lanterns he has prepared. In the middle of the meditation hall, backing Manjusri's shrine, is hung the big magic lantern which is the communal effort, depicting difficult or funny scenes from the monastic life, or other flights of fancy.

At this time of the year the rainy season is just about over and the real heat is beginning. For the evening meal, at which all expected visitors are present, lots of the thin buckwheat noodles so beloved in Japan as cooling summer fare are prepared, cooled in the kitchen well or on ice should some be available or sent in. The noodles are dipped in a cold sauce of soy beans, chopped spring onions, ground sesame seeds, and chopped fried bean curds – a real treat.

O Bon is a yearly family reunion, where the living and the dead come together again, a time of remembrance and festivity rather than of sadness.

The visitors arrive just before it gets dark; all are in some way connected with the monastery, either because their family graves are there, or they are neighbours and donors, or just well-wishers. And they bring their children.

It is the only time that the meditation hall is open to the public. Part of the floor is covered with the traditional red carpet, and a tea maker sits by a charcoal brazier with the kettle singing, ready to serve the sweet dainties and ceremonial tea. A joyous, festive spirit prevails.

As the visitors walk round admiring the decorations and lanterns, both children and adults indicate which lanterns they would like to take home with them. Red slips are stuck on by proud makers to indicate that they are already bespoken. Ideally, every single lantern is taken away, leaving 'nothing'.

Then it gets dark. The wooden block is struck as usual. The monks line up before the meditation platform, each at his place; the visitors take up places at the end of the hall. The Master approaches, as always conducted by the head monk. Entering the hall by the front entrance, he prostrates himself before Manjusri, is then handed a bundle of burning incense sticks, steps up on to the platform and, moving from place to place, puts a lighted incense stick before each tablet while the monks chant. As soon as he has done the round, he leaves the hall. At that, the bespoken lanterns may be removed, the noodles are served in the refectory, and by 8.30 p.m. all is over. The monks clear up, have their share of noodles, the discipline is relaxed, and they enjoy a social evening.

The end of July is the Great Sesshin with which the Summer Retreat comes to an end. This is a rather cruel one on account of the heat and mosquitoes. The last day of it is again the formal end ceremony which follows the same pattern as the one with which the retreat began. The last Teisho being given, the High Seat is removed from the shrine room. By midday all is cleared away, and the Sesshin continues until the evening. After the last formal interviews are over, at about 8.30 p.m., tea is served in the meditation hall, as always after Sanzen, but at the end of a Sesshin there is a longer break followed by only a short sitting period and early bed time. Next morning the monks are allowed to sleep in until about 6 a.m.

This is followed by a week or ten days' relaxed discipline with which the between period starts. During this week, all the offices change. Head monk, Zendo head monk, and head cook change offices and quarters. Among the younger monks the Master's attendant, the monk who leads the Sutra chanting, and the cook helper also change, so that each monk for half a year learns one by one the different tasks.

The two head monks, the head cook, and the Master's attendant have private quarters, the latter in the vicinity of the Master's quarters so as to be available at all times. The rest sleep in the meditation hall.

Also during this period some of the monks may go on leave, usually to their Dharma Father, though the older ones may also visit their parents or travel. Should their Dharma Father be short-handed for the preparations for the forthcoming public O Bon celebrations in mid-August, he may keep the monk to help him and only send him back to the monastery afterwards.

The in-between summer term is also a busy time in the monastery. Formal and kitchen gardens need a lot of attention, sweeping, weeding and pruning as does the cemetery; this is also the time for repair works. The days are long, and work sometimes continues till it gets dark. The 'medicinal meal' is late and the monks are tired out and are allowed to turn in early.

Also, the monks may supply a source of labour for donors and be invited to cut trees or pick tea, and other tasks. They may then keep a share of the wood and will certainly bring back the roots to use for fuel and the coarse tea leaves which they dry and roast for their tea. The bath is heated by a wood fire and the kitchen also uses wood; a great deal of sawing and chopping is always necessary. The kitchen garden also needs a lot of work; though the planting and sowing is usually the task of the head cook, the digging, hoeing and weeding are done by the community.

The skilful pruning of shrubs and trees in the formal gardens is an expert job which the monks have to learn. Inside and outside the monastery compound there is the never-ending sweeping up of leaves from the many trees, as well as the needles from the pines which are prominent in every Japanese garden.

Mid-September again brings an exceptionally busy time with preparations for the big equinox services which are again concerned with the dead, especially the recent dead. In preparation, gardens and grounds are meticulously cleaned, all flagstone paths and wooden gangways are washed, tea houses and annexes made spick and span, as well as special cleaning of the main buildings. Hundreds of guests are expected, and will be served with food. All the lacquerware is taken out and washed in advance. Cooking preparations are under way during the previous day for the traditional vegetarian banquet.

Though monks may eat, and indeed are expected to eat, outside what is given them, the rule is that neither flesh nor fish must pass through the monastery gates. In a traditional monastery, monks are proud of their cooking, and the head cook shows skill and ingenuity to add a special touch to the traditional food and garnishings. Normally, the food is rather plain, but sufficient: rice, a vegetable and/or beancurd soup, and salt pickles prepared by the monks themselves. Indeed, one of the most popular Japanese pickles, made from the giant radish, was 'invented' in a monastery.

The afternoon before the ceremony, the shrine hall is garlanded with the festive banners, a large altar is set up before it, offerings are set out on it, tablets and flags inscribed and put up or hung around it.

When the day arrives, lay women come to help in the kitchen, particularly with the washing up and drying of the lacquer dishes; though the monastery keeps a large amount of them, the meals are usually served in two sittings to cope with the multitude. Each portion is set out on a lacquer tray, six bowls to a tray, four with lids – so over 100 guests make for a busy day!

The monks like these occasions: there is less discipline, they enjoy being hosts, and it is a chance for them to talk to lay people in an ordinary way, and hear their troubles. Though a monk has problems too, they are different from those of lay life. Once the monk becomes a priest, familiarity with the problems of lay life is important. But these contacts are also an encouragement for their chosen life.

The ceremony itself is rather short, attended by priests of nearby temples as well as by lay people. Sutras are chanted, the Master dedicates the altar; the names of all those who have died during the last year are read, offerings are made to the dead, the Master delivers a short sermon, more chanting, and then one by one, the Master, the other priests, the monks, and lay people, offer incense. With that, the ceremony is at an end.

Food is served by the monks, including a cup of Sake, or rice wine. When all the guests have gone, the monks and their helpers have their meal, clean up and by mid-afternoon all is back to normal. The rest of the day is a relaxed one for the monks. After this, the timetable shifts to winter schedule – rising at 4 a.m.

October the fifth is Bodhidharma's death anniversary. How it came to be fixed on this day is not known; like Christmas, such dates are established by tradition. They are days of commemoration, and after the ceremonial part is over the monks can relax.

One of the great occasions is Founder's Day, the death anniversary of the founder. The ceremony takes place in the shrine room, priests from neighbouring temples come as well as associated lay people. Led by the Master, priests and monks walk a special pattern during the Sutra chanting. And as always, a meal is afterwards served to all.

Food in the monastery is plain. However, there are times for the odd good meal too, though except for festive occasions, not in the monastery. In case of death or the remembrance day of a death, monks may be asked to come and read Sutras. The monks take this duty in turn and are always well fed afterwards and bring home a donation for the monastery. There is also the custom of inviting monks to a Dana meal, either the whole community or, if this is not possible on account of space or cost, a few monks at a time, but never one monk alone. Led by a senior monk, they walk there in single file; both inside and outside the monastery, the rules for deportment are strict. Upon arrival, they chant Sutras, and then are served a large meal, for the monks, especially the young ones, can have healthy appetites.

A joyous mood prevails during the meal, and Sake is usually served as well, but the limits of deportment are not overstepped.

Rinzai Zen is not overloaded with ritual; it serves the community as well as training monks in 'The Great Matter', the matter of life and death. But though there is a minimum of ritual, the rules for deportment are strict, and the day is punctuated by religious observances, of which Sutra chanting is the main one. The monks have to learn the Sutras by heart. The meaning of the Sutras is not considered when chanting; each Sutra has a different melody and rhythm. The monks chant with full voices and open throats. One needs to have done it oneself in chorus to realise that good chanting is an effective emptying of the chattering mind, as well as stirring something deep in the heart – for when the mind is stilled, the heart is open.

Whatever Sutras are chanted, they invariably end with the

three times repeated chanting of the Four Great Vows:

Sentient Beings are numberless,
I vow to be of assistance to all for their awakening;
The deluding passions are inexhaustible,
I vow to work them all out;
The Dharma gates are manifold,
I vow to learn them all;
The Buddha Way is supreme,
I vow to tread it to the end.

I have often heard Westerners voice an objection to those vows on the following lines: How can I vow such a thing? Even with complete dedication, how could I dare to vow such an undertaking? From our basic assumptions this seems a fair objection; but it does not hold. Of course, I alone, that illusory and deluded I whose very existence is denied in the Buddhist teaching, cannot expect to fulfil such a vow.

There is a Dutch sailing proverb: 'God helps the sailor, but he must steer himself.' Both sides are always involved – but this is difficult for us to understand, and even more so to act in accordance with; that one must go full out, not stint oneself, but know also that there are limits to what one can do. If I acknowledge those limits but nevertheless do my utmost (this will be discussed later under 'total effort', p. 127, somehow the other side comes to help.

This is why the Easterner makes these vows. He knows he cannot keep them, they are too great. But he can do his utmost, and that he vows to do; by that he evokes the helping hand of Kannon Bosatsu, the Bodhisattva of compassion and deliverance, to help the undertaking; this link is established just by the dedication, the vows. It is precisely this which makes the Four Great Vows so momentous, so all-important. Hence they are chanted again and again.

In mid-October the Winter Retreat begins with its opening ceremony and Great Sesshin. As the days get darker, the evening sitting is ever longer during the winter term. At the beginning of November the monks change into winter robes. There is no heating in the monastery, and though warm underwear is worn, bare feet on the straw mats and wooden gangways, and straw sandals or wooden clogs on bare feet out of doors, make conditions rather hard. At about this time the annual begging tour into the country takes place for the giant radishes which the monks pickle themselves.

Teisho, begging a few times a week, and every fifth day bathing, shaving, and doing the laundry; the usual work of sweeping leaves outside and inside the grounds, chopping wood, cleaning, garden work; time never drags in the monastery. As December approaches, the forthcoming Rohatsu Great Sesshin begins to exercise the minds of all in the monastery, and the new monks approach it with apprehension.

In the Mahayana school, the Buddha's day of Enlightenment is celebrated on the eighth of December. As the legend has it, having settled himself down under the Bo-tree with the resolution not to get up until he had seen through his problems, it was on the morning of the eighth of December that Gotama looked up, saw the morning star and became the Enlightened One, the Buddha.

In memory of that occasion, the monks dedicate the week from the first of December to the morning of the eighth to supreme effort, following to the limit of their ability the great example of the Buddha.

Extra food supplies are begged beforehand, the grounds are swept of leaves, a large amount of wood for the kitchen fires is sawn and split, and all necessary preparations are made; work stops during this Sesshin except in the kitchen. The afternoon before the monks have a few hours to go out, and they use this to go shopping for supplies. That evening, the monastery gates are closed as usual for the night, and they are not opened again until the eighth of December. There is the ceremonial tea with the Master, and traditionally it is understood that, as the Buddha vowed not to get up, so the monks will undertake to die rather than give up their attempt to break through the ignorance of I.

Somehow Rohatsu always coincides with the first real cold and frost. All sliding doors and windows are wide open, the winds whistle through the monastery in the long evening sittings, and the cold penetrates the early morning sittings. The time schedule is hard; the monks rise at 2 a.m. and except for meal times, tea served in the meditation hall, daily Teisho, and four Sanzen interviews a day, Zazen prevails. The food is good. And there is one treat, something to look forward to when everything seems to have reached rock bottom, a little ray of warmth beckoning. At 10 p.m. just as the cold seems to penetrate one's marrow, boiling hot, spicy noodle soup is served in the refectory, as much as each can eat.

This description may sound odd to the reader in a reasonably warm room, reasonably well fed, and reasonably free to do as he wishes. To appreciate fully what this sudden gift means one needs the living experience, not necessarily even a Rohatsu Sesshin, but of being absolutely and completely reduced, exhausted, with no redress and no letup, at the same time making one's utmost effort – as Master Hakuin expressed it, enduring what is unendurable. Getting up, moving one's cramped legs, stretching them on the way to the refectory. Bowing, sitting down, and then receiving the heavenly bowl of piping hot food, at first uncertain whether one should nurse it to warm one's numb hands or get it inside where it begins to glow and radiate warmth all through one's body. Never have I eaten better noodles, nor will I, than those Rohatsu ones, they are legendary, too; and the monks' eyes shine when they talk about it any time of the year.

Rohatsu Sesshin is a grim Sesshin, and lest one forgets, it reminds one that this Great Matter is truly a matter of life and death. A little bit of I dies every Rohatsu. The monks are without heat, and cannot bath, or shave, and on the last day they look haggard but determined.

The last day also sees a change in the daily routine. Teisho is in the afternoon, and afterwards all go and clean the immediate grounds. All the leaves that fell during the last week have been piling up knee deep, and are now swept together into huge piles and burnt; this is hard and fast work, but a welcome relief to muscles cramped with cold and long sitting. Then back into the meditation hall.

The last night is sat through. There is also a last, very formal Sanzen at midnight. A cup of rice dregs is served afterwards in memory of the Buddha's accepting a cup of milk gruel before he sat himself down for his supreme effort, his resolve strengthening the monks' endeavour.

About 3 a.m. on the morning of the eighth of December, the sitting comes to a formal end. The Zendo head monk addresses the community; the bath is heated. Head monk, Zendo head monk, and lay sitters have a hot snack in the head monk's office, usually sweet bean sauce with rice dumplings, followed by the thick ceremonial tea. But soon the Zendo head monk is called; the bath is hot, and in person he tenderly scrubs the backs of his monks, loosening the muscles. Many a young monk overawed by this bursts into tears.

The eighth of December is the Buddha's Enlightenment Day. The monks have little chance to sleep, for at 6 a.m. there is Sutra chanting to celebrate it. But for the rest of the day the discipline is relaxed.

With Rohatsu Sesshin over, the new monks are treated with less severity. They have been through the hardest time of the monastic year, and are now considered really established.

On the 22nd of December, the evening after the winter solstice, the turning from dark to light is celebrated. It is also known as the driving out of the evil spirit of resentment. That evening, there is a party in the monastery during which the order is reversed. The new monks are the guests, enjoy the seats of honour, and the old monks serve them. It is a gay party. At about 4 p.m. in the afternoon, a bonfire is lit in the yard around which the monks warm themselves; sweet potatoes are roasted in it and are eaten on the spot. The Master usually leaves the monastery for that night. The kitchen is busy preparing all sorts of goodies. A few lay people who have done long training there at various times are also invited. All bring Sake, the Japanese rice wine that is drunk heated, and on that evening it is freely served. The party takes place in the offices of the head monk. The new monks are served first, and are really feasted. Everybody is supposed to perform, a sketch on monastic life is the usual choice for the new monks; the older ones often portray the difficult stages in the life of the new monks, or some particular skill they have; the lay people also take part, often singing or dancing excerpts from Noh-plays. Classical and farcical skits and sketches intertwine, and the party goes with a swing. I remember vividly one chubby new monk with a really sweet disposition, more often than not in some sort of scrape, saucily enduring the scolding for it and taking it in his stride. He was made to take the part of the Master in a mock Sanzen interview. Seated on his cushion, blowing himself up, with the Keisaku in front of him, he looked in no way put out on seeing the dreaded old head monk creeping up to him perfectly portraying all the fear and hesitation of a new monk. Rather, he gave him a sounding whack with the Keisaku in best Sanzen style, and firmly shook the hand bell to show the interview as finished. Thus the party continues. Whether the monks like drinking or not, that evening everybody must drink his fill. By about 10.30 p.m. the party comes to an end. The young monks withdraw if they can, or are helped away. The head monks clear up, clean, sweep and wash up so that next morning the place is as spick and span as usual. And the young monks wake up later than usual: after such a changeover with its frolicsome joy, they usually feel that the dreaded old head monks who have been so fierce with them are human beings after all and really rather nice.

By that time, they have also ripened sufficiently to have some inkling of how important and formative a time they have had with this treatment. And so the evil spirits of resentment are driven out, symbolically just after the darkest time of the year, the winter solstice, when the darkness turns again towards the light.

In a way, this is also the graduation party of the new monks, who henceforth are treated as full monks in their second year.

As the year begins to draw to its end, the monastery, and indeed the whole of Japan, becomes active. From about the 27th, the evenings are spent in making slips and folders for the New Year decorations and gifts, and general preparations.

On the 29th the traditional making of rice dumplings takes place. It is very heavy but joyous work. The huge granite mortar standing waist-high is brought into the lower part of the kitchen. The rice is steamed in sets of screens over a cauldron, each screen holding one portion of rice for the pounding. When cooked, the steaming portion is transferred into the mortar and two monks pound it to a purée with huge wooden mallets. Then one monk continues the pounding until it is reduced to a very fine consistency. This pounding with the heavy mallets in an even but fast rhythm is backbreaking work. The monks take it in turn, and one stands by resting but counting to set the pace. Those who can keep going with the mallets for a maximum number of beats are greatly admired. But here, too, total effort, going all out, not holding back, is encouraged, and is more important than the actual achievement. For even consistency, the dough has to be turned frequently; this is done by another monk, quickly turning the hot dough between the beats. A bucket with cold water stands by to cool the almost scalded hands; this, too, is done in turn, but needs great skill to avoid serious injury.

Lay people come to help, young strong men with the pounding, others in the actual shaping of the dough. A spirit of joy and zest prevails; each going full out in that total effort which really cannot be stressed too much, and which is as important in the everyday tasks as it is in the sitting. But a friendly, social mood prevails and the discipline is easy.

On the floor of the kitchen proper a huge board is laid out, like an enormous pastry board, and on this the various sized dumplings are formed, dusted with rice flower and set aside to cool. This, especially for the large ones, is skilful work as they are then left to dry and are stored to be used over the next few months. If any air is left inside they go mouldy.

Usually a crate of tangerines is delivered for that day by some sponsor or greengrocer, for all to eat as and when they please. As a snack halfway through the morning, the new, still moist and hot dumplings are served in a mixture of grated radish and soy sauce, and also as a sweet. By mid-afternoon all has been finished and cleared up. The monks have a much needed bath and rest for the day.

The 30th and 31st of December see a thorough and complete cleaning, washing and sweeping. By the late evening of the 31st all must be ready.

As midnight approaches, the bell-tower monk takes his place at the big bell over the gate and at midnight gives the first boom. Bells are struck from outside by means of a horizontal beam suspended on ropes with a pulling rope attached to it. The interval between each boom is the length of a very quick chanting of the Heart Sutra, about two minutes. One hundred and eight booms are sounded; it is said that there are 108 passions, and one is expelled by each boom, so that everybody may start the New Year with a clean slate.

Lay people also come along. All is very quiet. The bell-tower is dimly lit. The head monk is usually about in the grounds. People enter through the gate, bow to the head monk, and exchange the traditional New Year's greeting: 'It has opened! Congratulations!' Then, lining up their footwear, one by one they climb up the ladder to the bell-tower, take their place, edging along until it is their turn to strike the bell, descend again and leave.

The ushering in of the New Year is a quiet time; no revelry takes place, no loud words are spoken. In that silence the booms of the temple bells far and near herald in the New Year.

For the monks New Year's Day starts early. The chanting of the Great Prajnaparamita Sutra takes place. This Sutra cannot be read through in one go as it is far too long; but since Sutra books are traditionally folded, the 'reading' consists in the main of opening these books rather like a concertina, and throwing them into a kind of wheel, page after page unfolding, and settling itself on the other side as read, while the sonorous chanting repeats again and again 'The Great Wisdom Gone Beyond'.

For three days there is little discipline in the monastery. There is very little cooking as the traditional New Year's food has been prepared in advance. The monks can take it easy, apart from looking after the visitors who come for the traditional New Year's visit, who are then served tea and given a little 'Christmas box'. However, rising is early for the chanting of the Great Prajnaparamita Sutra which takes place on three consecutive mornings.

The tenth of January is the anniversary of Master Rinzai's death. (Master Rinzai was the 'Father' of the Rinzai School.)[5] This is another easy day in the monastery. After this the second

5. *The Record of Rinzai* (The Buddhist Society 1975).

half of the Winter Retreat gets into gear. The mid-retreat Great Sesshin in mid-January falls into the 'Great Cold' period, and is very hard on that account. The second week in February brings the end-retreat Great Sesshin with the usual closing ceremony.

This is followed by a week's relaxation, and the usual change of office among the oldest monks. The day of the Buddha's death anniversary falls during this week on the 15th of February. On the evening of the 13th, the big Nirvana hanging scroll is hung in front of the main Buddha image in the shrine room, and on the morning of the 15th a special Sutra chanting takes place. After that monks due for leave may depart, but they are usually back again by the end of February.

The third week of March is very busy with preparations for the spring equinox, equivalent to the autumn one. From then on, the time changes to summer schedule. The new applicants begin to arrive, begging for admission.

The eighth of April is the Buddha's birthday. An image of the infant Buddha is washed with sweet tea, flowers decorate temples and images, Sutras are chanted, and the festival is one of joy and gratitude.

With that, the monastic year has gone full circle. Indeed, there is always something just about to start, something to look forward to or something to brace oneself for, and though there are moments and times when things seem to last for an eternity, by and large the monastic year passes very swiftly. I remember once jokingly saying to the head monk: 'I wonder whether time in Japan passes faster?' He remarked with a big grin: 'Are you sure? Perhaps it is time in the monastery.'

How is the new monk affected by his first year? After the initial settling in during the Summer Retreat, the respite during the in-between term, then the hard Winter Retreat, a perceptible change has taken place, particularly noticeable after Rohatsu week. The change is more than just being licked into shape superficially, it is a change in depth, a real and unmistakable solidification of personality. For that, the first year is crucial, and the harshness and hardness with which the young monks are treated are the formative factor.

During the second year, a great deal of lenience is extended, individual lines emerge during that time and can develop. The third year is again hard and brings things to a crunch. During this year the monk finds his real vocation – either staying on for long-term training or leaving to take over a temple of his own. By now he has been through most of the usual tasks allotted to new monks. Also during his second or third year, the monk becomes for a term the Master's attendant. The change that takes place in the monk during that period needs to be seen to be believed. It is one of the really formative factors, and known to be so. The solidity which has been acquired during the first year is strengthened further but is now also tempered by a gentleness and adaptability which marks the first step towards the state of 'sitting light' and 'riding circumstances rather than being driven by them', which is stressed in the Rinzai school.

The fourth and fifth years are usually difficult ones. Those who get over the restlessness of that time and stay and settle down to the long haul of training become the elder monks responsible for the order and the running of the monastery. A very few will finish their personal training, and after a quiet period be called to become Master of a monastery.

The symbol of the wholeness of The Way (Tao) shows the primal pair of opposites curled up in a circle, with each containing the seed or eye of the other. A traditional monastery also shows two faces. To see the monks sitting in the meditation hall is to a newcomer somewhat awe-inspiring, and may even evoke fear; total effort, controlled, because contained in a form, is great strength. In us, the emotions usually slop around or are so repressed that we are only half alive. The strength resulting from the transformation impresses by its very presence. But that alone would soon become rigid. And so to balance it there is the joyful or playful aspect during times of relaxed discipline. And finally, there are the work periods which allow the monks to ponder their problems as well as to contain them.

What actually happens depends on the monk himself. No training method is a sausage machine from which the finished product emerges neatly packed. There is also much talk nowadays about the need for modernisation or, here, for westernisation. But this is beside the point, for the emotions, derived from instinctual energy, are as old as life. The way to transform them is the same as of old, the same in East, or West, North or South. The traditional training ways, of which the Zen Way is one, have centuries of experience of dealing with human nature, and of guiding along the way to the heart. It is not an easy way, and it is said that in walking it, it 'behoves one to seek good friends'; guides that help when obstacles loom, and suggest ways how to overcome them.

Though the activities of the Zen Way can be described, these are but pictures. However descriptive a picture of the life in a Zen monastery may be, it does not and cannot touch the essential point, which is what concretely happens in the trainee. What can be described is only the framework. Again, we are reminded of the Zen warning not to mistake the pointing finger for the moon.

The same applies to the reading of Zen texts. Quite a few are translated. From a superficial reading we gain nothing, or misunderstand. When Master Rinzai tells his monks to 'kill the Buddha when they meet him' – we, to whom the Buddha means little, are rather pleased with such iconoclastic statements. We hardly stop to think what such a statement might mean to a monk who has devoted his life to the Buddha. Perhaps this passage, translated idiomatically for us, should read: 'If you meet your ingrained opinions, your dearest ideal without which life has no meaning for you – kill it.' Yes, this is the awesome task with which that hard crust of I that encases the warm human heart is finally broken, and upon that its inherent warmth flows of itself, shedding light all round. And with that emerges the deep sense of gratitude.

Here in the West, Buddhism, and Zen, are often thought cold, and this not only because of the misreading as 'mind' for 'heart' but because we are object-oriented. To just feel grateful is not enough for our strong and wilful Western I. This I conceives of gratitude only for something received, and is at best short-lived, and all too easily turns into either demand or resentment; or it is felt for somebody who is favouring *me,* equally quickly changing or exhausted. Real gratitude is a quality of the heart, as is love. It needs no object, because the subject, I, is also missing. Perhaps its nearest equivalent in the West comes, not surprisingly, from the Christian mystics who describe it as 'feeling like walking under a cloud of grace'.

No religion or religious training can afford to bypass the heart. If it does it ceases to be a religion and it no longer warms or nourishes. If the Zen Way, which is a Buddhist Way, is to take root and to grow in our soil, it will need the nurture suggested in one of its basic tenets: 'A direct transmission from heart to heart.' Growth needs warmth; only heart can touch heart and incite unfoldment.

Little has been said about the role of the Master. He is the heart of the monastery. He is always there. The part he plays in the training has been described, however, elsewhere.[6]

Though the relation between him and his monks, indeed all training under him, is binding, he is not a Guru in the Indian sense. Perhaps his most outstanding characteristic is sheer solidity. He may seem aloof to somebody trying to throw out a projection line – for he has no hooks on which the line can engage. It is this which makes him a Master.

6. Irmgard Schloegl, *The Wisdom of the Zen Masters* (Sheldon Press 1975).

FUNDAMENTALS

Bodhidharma, an Indian monk, is said to have brought the Zen School to China. Whether historical or not, the quatrain traditionally attributed to him sums up the essence of the Zen School:

'A special transmission outside the teachings;
Not standing on written words or letters.
Direct pointing to the human heart,
Seeing into its nature and becoming Buddha.'

Flowers bloom and wither. One of the basic tenets of Buddhism is that all changes. But the deluded I clings to fixtures as a safety anchor. Being itself nothing, it needs to have some-thing, physical and/or mental possessions, both to prove its existence to itself and to incorporate more and more 'insatiably' for its security. Since this process is limited, because no I can incorporate or possess the world, this is a fruitful source of hurt and frustration, that unease which the Buddha found fundamental as the basic delusion.

When the living spirit leaves the word, the word becomes rigid, an empty husk. When the living spirit is forgotten in an exposition that it has forged, the formulation becomes dead language to which the mind clings and which it seeks to interpret. As to that, the ironical question of the Zen Masters through the ages is: 'What juice do you think you can suck from dry bones?'

The Zen School does not deny the scriptures and its Masters are deeply versed in them, but they do not countenance clinging to mere words and fashioning shortsighted interpretations. They insist on the cultivation of the living spirit. Thus the first two lines of the quatrain.

The Zen School holds itself as the Buddha Heart School. It says of itself that it is a transmission from heart to heart. It is concerned with the heart, and the last two lines of the quatrain show this concern. They point directly to the human heart, and the Zen Way is to follow this pointing and to see into the nature of the human heart, which is one's own heart, and so to become Buddha, awakened.

Hui Neng, the sixth Chinese patriarch, after whom the Zen School becomes Chinese, says that the essence of the heart is intrinsically pure. Two frequent analogies for it are the bright mirror, and the brilliantly clear, cold winter moon. Pondering these analogies, we may look along the pointing finger to where it actually points.

The brilliantly cold winter moon. That which is intrinsically pure, shines of its own nature. That we can see. But why cold? When Love/Compassion is the very nature of the heart, and Wisdom its function? And the Buddha is called the All-Compassionate One? How can it be possible? The heart, intrinsically pure, shines of its own nature. However, this shining purity is overcast by the cloud of basic delusion from which every I suffers. Thus, it is not perceptible to I, which stands to reason, for I is but a bundle of delusions and appetites, in itself non-existing. Since we all know to our cost what havoc, misery and suffering these delusions and appetites can and do create, we may simply say that with I, and as long as the delusion of such a separate I lasts, there clings an aspect of primitive wildness to the heart which is in need of taming, gentling, and transforming to that which it is by nature. I experience these appetites – whether material or mental – as compelling, a hot flame. The passions are red. Deliverance from them, which is also deliverance from I, is bound to be portrayed by its opposite. Hence the murky heat of blind passion is contrasted with the brilliantly clear, cold winter moon.

The bright mirror. Hui Neng already mentions the great mirror wisdom of the heart. This heart mirror is the uncluttered shining surface – it reflects truly what confronts it, without distortion or discoloration. Nor does it cling to a reflection that has fallen into it. If the reflected object moves or the mirror turns, it lets it go.

In itself, the mirror has no colour, and so it can reflect all colours. And since it contains nothing, its surface is smooth and bright; so it can reflect all things just as they are. This mirror is not concerned with forms; it merely reflects what falls into it. That is, when it is turned outwards, towards the world.

And when it is turned inwards? It can by now hardly be surprising that then it reflects nothing – for it only reflects what is, and there is no I. This is the true empty heart – *mushin*. It is the source of all energy, responding freely; when turned outwards and meeting phenomena it reflects them; when turned inwards, it is empty, at rest.

These two analogies serve to bring into focus the truth that 'heart' in Buddhist terminology stands for a totality that must forever be foreign to I. This is fortunate, for in both its full functioning and in its emptiness it would frighten I out of its wits. Nor am I capable of doing anything to bring this about, for the heart is inherent anyway. I am but the distorting factor, and whatever I do intentionally, serves only as further distortion. Yet, if I do nothing, the old delusion continues.

The Zen Way starts, as it were, on the horns of this dilemma. By now, we have at least an inkling of what it entails (see above pp. 15-17, 'I want something', etc.). The question is how can this transformation be brought about.

To help us, we have the example of the Buddha, how he courageously faced his problems and suffered them out. 'Suffering I teach, and the Way out of Suffering' – not by futile attempts at evasion, but by courageously facing one's problems till they are suffered through. With that, the creator of problems, I, with its sticky attachments and aversions, is also changed. To I, always itching to do, interfere, meddle, this sounds negative and passive. Hence Master Rinzai said 1,000 years ago that the ordinary man does not naturally take to it; and Master Hakuin warned that to walk this way means to be prepared to sweat white beads, for it entails bearing what is unbearable and enduring what is unendurable.

The Zen Way can be described as regards its form, but the important thing to keep firmly in mind is that such description is misleading. A description of a process is always mechanistic, and the living process is anything but a mechanical system. It may seem so from the outside, and there has always been the danger of its being mistaken for it. One of the earliest Zen texts, the 'Sutra of Hui Neng', already stresses this point, on which the controversy between this line and the mechanical mirror wiping of the Northern line arose. The latter became extinct within a few generations. Into a mechanical approach inevitably there creeps in the bugbear of I doing it, I progressing through the stages, I attaining to what I want, by my willpower. And just this I is denied in Buddhism; in a thoroughly practical training it is outgrown.

If the heart is empty of clinging or aversion, of the *emotions* which are the film of delusion engendered by I, this is the heart's fulfilment. This is basic to Zen practice which takes the heart as empty unless or until the winds of passion stir up emotional waves.

Hence a strong component of Zen practice is the practice in everyday life, *shugyo,* without which Zazen practice cannot be fruitful. It is the practice in everyday life, the ordinary work, which makes the student come to grips with his emotionality. Again, Hui Neng already warned against only sitting quietly and another Zen story, that a brick cannot be polished into a mirror, illustrates the same point. If Zen teaches anything, it is the ability to be vitally alive. The heart being empty, hence fulfilled, there is a free and adequate response to changing situations.

Too much method robs the life. Too much analysis clutters the mind with details. The dogmatic forms of religion are manifold. Their training ways have much in common. And the mystics of all ages speak much the same language.

One is apt to get lost in a welter of forms or, as the proverb has it, not to see the wood for the trees. It is peculiarly difficult for us to see both sides of a question or of an argument, for we are by nature one-sided, inclining more to this than to that. It is even more difficult to see the same thing as both this and that, the same yet not the same. Much of the later training along the Zen Way is concerned with this, though unspoken to begin with, it is fundamental. In this chapter we shall deal with fundamentals.

No two leaves of the same oak are exactly alike. No two oaks are exactly alike. But they are beyond doubt oak trees, and oak leaves. All of them. From an acorn will grow an oak. We know it; it seems commonplace.

Prototypes and collective concepts are abstractions in our mind to facilitate our understanding. Factually, they do not exist. And yet, things are in conformity with them. What abstractions really try to express is the nature of things; we can say of an oak that it has leaves of distinctive shape, etc., and that its seeds will grow into like trees. So they are the same *and* individually different from each other; and not the same *and* collectively different from what is other than oak. Although we know this applies also to us human beings, we easily lose the awareness of being the same when confronted with others individually different from us or me.

We in the West have lost our spiritual values since our age of enlightenment and are now unfamiliar with spiritual development. What meets the eye is the first thing to be seen; it need not be the essential. There is much talk today of 'religious experience', descriptions of such, even whole systems of classification. 'Enlightenment' has almost become a catchphrase, everybody projecting into the term what he feels most lacking, thus seeing in it a beckoning and almost magical fulfilment. Such hopes are based on the delusion from which we all, every I, suffer.

The message of the Buddha, as appropriate today as it ever was, is a rather hard and demanding one, but one that is concretely feasible. It requires more than an experience of ecstasy, which as such, whatever its length or frequency, is not productive of a real change of heart, a transformation of energy and thus a restructuring of the total man as a result of a new way of seeing. This 'clear seeing' is a change of attitude, and as such, is the first step with which training begins; as the developed clarity, it finally results in genuine insight into one's own nature, which is that of man.

Thus two points emerge:

1. This genuine insight is not mere intellectual understanding, for it involves also the emotional factors. It is doctrinally expressed as 'the single eye'.
2. For just this reason it is not possible for an I to have this insight. Hence, the restructuring process is not something that I can undertake; it takes place of itself, is a move of nature to correct habitual lop-sidedness, and constitutes a becoming whole.

The difficulty, especially for a self-conscious, self-assertive and hence aggressive-destructive Western I, is to set such a process in motion without I having the planning and controlling upper hand.

The first step along that path is self-discipline. I, by nature one-sided, will either fight shy of discipline on the principle that it does not suit me; or I will load on an arbitrary discipline which I either cannot keep in the long run – or the life spark is lost in hypocrisy, a sullen smouldering under the ashes.

A discipline that is not I-controlled is inconceivable to I. Yet, most of the physiological processes that go on in my body are not I-controlled. Hair and nails grow, the heart pumps, the lungs function of themselves. Worse, moods seize me, passions rise and can carry me away, whether I know it, like it, resist it, or not. If I wake up in the morning with a heavy heart, I may blame my liver or the weather for it – but there need not be a physical reason at all, only a heavy, bleak mood has invaded me, has taken possession of me; not being 'mine', I cannot shake it off. It will leave me again sooner or later of its own accord. Usually I try to find a scapegoat so that I know what caused it; and if I cannot remedy this cause, I can at least blame the scapegoat, and feel secure in the knowledge that it has nothing to do with me. Or else I try to distract myself in order to shake off the mood. The last thing I want to do is to endure it willingly, and accept it as a part of myself which is in a state of agitation, I know not why; and which if only I endure it patiently, will leave me sooner or later, I do not know why.

Having been courageous and honest enough to have seen this happen time and again, the inevitable conclusion must be that I am at least sharing the 'house' I live in, of which I thought myself the master, with something unknown, something stronger than I, and acting in a way which seems to me to be without rhyme or reason.

My disquiet upon finding such a mate is bound to be serious. This is why I prefer not to be aware of him, and go to great lengths to avoid seeing him. Unfortunately in turning my back so as not to see him, I actually give him special power over me. For the stronger I resist something the more that something fascinates me, gets hold of me. This repulsion is of the same power as the attraction of 'I want something' (p. 26), but its opposite pole.

'Suffering I teach and the Way out of suffering.' Why do we want to undertake such a practice? And what do we expect to get out of it? Some such considerations are prompting us whether we know it or not.

Traditionally it is said that there are three stages in the Zen Training. The first is Hearing with the Ear, and for us Westerners this might idiomatically be rendered as 'Reading with the Eye'. If sufficiently attracted by what we read/hear we begin to mull it over, think about it, try to find out more, thus we reach the second stage of Pondering in the Heart; and this is then followed by the third stage of Practice with the Body.

There is also the warning that should the third stage be delayed or shirked, the Pondering moves from the heart to the head and there gives rise to fantastic speculations. These are the 'flowers in the empty sky', idle vanity which does not quicken and is seen as an illness.

Thus, from the outset three things are needed to make training possible; a great root of faith; a great root of doubt, and fierce determination. For us in the West, reared in a different cultural climate, we might add two more: great patience; and great honesty – both applied to oneself.

Bearing in mind that the Zen Way is a Buddhist way, we may expect it to concentrate on the basic principles, the awakening of the realisation of Not-I, by means of a genuine transformation of the emotional household. For I and emotions are closely connected though, paradoxically, also mutually exclusive – enemies who nevertheless go arm in arm.

I am a complex bundle of wants and dislikes, hopes and fears. I experience myself through this bundle of reactions to an object other than I. All aspirations, altruistic intentions, sly evasions, dear opinions and ideals, also belong to this complex, which is 'fired' into action by the emotions.

The novice in the temple, and later on when he becomes a monk in a training monastery, though his life is much harder, settles in; once the initial strangeness and novelty are dispelled, his life becomes as much routine as our work-a-day life is to us. But the monk has no choice. He is there of his own choice but while there he has chosen to accept the discipline as it exists: complete obedience, a hard life, simple food, curtailed sleep, little rest. And, of course, he must participate in the religious observances, and the meditation sittings. He has no way out, his day is structured from waking to sleeping.

Though we also have a work-a-day life with our established routine, within it we have considerable leeway and can shift things as it suits us. When this liberty is infringed we tend to react strongly. We are usually inclined to think we have little freedom, limited by the necessity of earning our living, and wanting much more freedom to do what we like.

The monk in his strict environment learns to take things as they come and to adapt quickly to changes of circumstance. He has already had a considerable amount of training in this as a novice and has, to an extent, learned to face and endure his emotional reactions. Of course, he is prey to emotions but he cannot throw a temper, nor huddle in a corner to fulminate inwardly, but has to function in the normal routine; knowing that he is there of his own free will and for his own training, something is forged in him, restructuring him. A good part of his daily work consists of sweeping indoors and outdoors and weeding. Silence is kept during the working hours and there is little talking except at odd moments. So the monk weeding, pulling out one weed after another, though he is boiling within, suffers the emotional onslaught, enduring it willy-nilly, almost dumbly but continues to function. He stops when the signals are given, starts the next job as and when required, saying 'yes' to whatever he is told and doing it as well as he can. It seems as if such a regime is more likely to produce an automaton or a dyed-in-the-wool hypocrite. But this is not so; enduring and working through the emotional onslaughts, 'suffering it out', serves a twofold purpose. If done in the attitude of training, willingly yet fully acknowledging the emotional upheaval, I who must have things as it suits me, become softer and more tractable as I learn again and again to give in, and to give in for no other reason than that the training requires it. To that extent the energy itself sloughs off its wildness and becomes 'more like itself'; as it is when not interfered with and misused by I. As a working model it might almost be seen as a two-way trigger effect: if I could be considered as a spiky ball (compare also p. 122) the spikes are then the impetuous spearheads of 'I must have', 'I need', 'I can't stand', 'I won't have', 'I am right'. These spikes act as thorns in my flesh, causing pain. The only relief would be the removal of the thorns. Unfortunately they cannot be pulled out but they can be ground away; the grinding agent is the emotional energy if allowed to rise without escaping. Only then can it conducively work as motor energy, which by its action is itself transformed. Hence the double process.

This analogy also serves to show why neither repression nor expression is effective in removing the spikes. Repression only dams up the energy until it finally exceeds the limit of tolerance and explodes in a primitive temper. And expression, though it may bring momentary relief from tension, is not a transforming agent; moreover, if habitually indulged in, it lowers the limit of tolerance and so works the opposite way. Instead of becoming gentler, for example, the person becomes more irascible.

It is important to notice one further point in this process of energy transformation and restructuring. The energy must have a fairly high potential to grind the spikes away and to be able to shift gear itself, as it were. This puts considerable stress on the container, the person undergoing training. Hence it is necessary for the container to be strong enough before such a shift can occur safely.

In any sport training is necessary to strengthen the muscles, and practice in skill of performance. The same holds good for 'inner strength'. Zen training starts with the ordinary person wishing to undergo it. Little by little, the practice is increased.

The novice in the temple learns to function in adverse circumstances, in difficulties he did not know, much less endure, at home. The entrance begging in the training monastery is a very real test, and a formative one.

Since the form is important, great stress is put on correct posture not only for Zazen but for deportment in general. There is little opportunity to do 'as it suits me'. Walking is straight, sitting is straight, standing is straight. A sloppy, lolling posture, physically or mentally, is not allowed. And yet, stiffness is also discouraged, physically and mentally. The form must be strong and firm, but flexible enough to stand the pressure as it builds up, to contain the shift when it occurs and to accommodate the new structure.

Immediately, the question arises, what is this shift? From computer programming we know that it is important to ask the 'right question' to produce the right answer from the information available. There is also a Zen saying that the answer is in the question. If we can find out what this shift is then we will also know why and how it occurs and that there can be a wrong shift or dislocation as well as a right shift or incorporation. As always, analogies help.

Though the shift seems always to occur suddenly and anything may seem to trigger it off, viz. the many Zen stories about it, in fact this is not so. These Zen stories present highlights, and are a kind of familiar shorthand note for a familiar process. We have been fascinated by them because to us the process is not familiar. Indeed, the process has attracted much attention and research in recent years, attempting from one angle or another to find out what so-called 'experiences' are, not only in the field of religion, for psychologists and behaviour researchers have also found facets of it. Provided we do not cling to the facet we have just 'discovered' and are not too carried away by that attraction to see it as the whole – which is good Buddhism as well as good science – we can quite readily discuss it.

A sudden shift has forerunners, little loosenings up that occur to prepare the way in which the shift can take place without disruption. This is very important. A gardener creates favourable conditions for his plants to grow. They grow themselves – he cannot do it for them – but if the conditions are unfavourable, the plants are retarded and warped or if forced, they are weak, and wither at the first cold blast.

The gardener is a man. He uses his knowledge and experience of plants and of their way of growing. If he is too impatient or too greedy for results or profit he interferes with the natural growth cycles rather than furthering them – so we have hot-house flowers that last a day, vegetables that hardly taste, exhausted soil, pollution problems and a movement back to organic growing which is unlikely to supply the needs of our technological mass society and its population explosion. In short, man has learned something of the processes of nature and adapted this knowledge exclusively to his needs, benefit and profit, in sovereign disregard for everything else. But man has also proved himself capable of being a good gardener and, as we know, man is capable of learning. Whether he will or will not learn depends on him.

Whether what we have learned of the processes of nature will ultimately be beneficial to us or not, also depends on us. Atomic fission is a tremendous source of energy; whether we use it to produce heat, light, 'power' to work for us, or whether we misuse it to produce destructive atom bombs depends on us, the users, and not on atomic fission which is merely what it is. We tend to forget that. Of all the processes of nature, we have concentrated on the 'objective' and ignored the 'subjective', ourselves, and now find ourselves rather like the sorcerer's apprentice – wary, uneasily staring ahead at what we have conjured up.

So, it also depends on us whether we are willing to take stock of what we know and become wise husbandmen, or whether we allow ourselves to be carried away by selfish greed, incapable of guiding our physical or mental lusts. Thus, it is also up to us whether we grow into what will prove to be a wild shoot of the tree of life, disregarding all other forms of life – and no doubt in time become extinct – or whether we can learn to contain ourselves and have true regard for all that lives. This does not consist of reducing everything to the lowest common denominator, thus robbing all forms of their birthright which is being other or different. We have outgrown the childish stage of innocence where the knowledge of good and evil yet slumbered in primordial identity; in the light of our consciousness we see differences. But perhaps the first thing to become aware of is our own insatiable wants and appetites that have nearly ravaged the earth we live on and our disregard for all forms of life other than 'mine'.

We have learned an enormous amount about the natural processes. This need not make us swollen-headed, thinking we 'control' nature; we do not control nature, we merely make use of its laws. We often misuse them, running greedily after short-term profits and indulging ourselves to our hearts' discontent. Nobody can deny the untold and very real benefits which this knowledge has brought us. The field of medicine is a good example. It also illustrates that it is apt to turn to ashes in our impious hands. And, if we pause to consider, we may realise that it is not our knowledge of the processes of nature which is to blame, but we ourselves, for we do not make intelligent use of this knowledge but grossly misuse it by greedy interference and total disregard of our also being subject to those laws. We foolishly set ourselves apart and hold ourselves 'above' them. Such swollen-headed blindness is bound to lead to catastrophes, for indeed it is asking to play at being God Almighty.

Such might be a present-day rephrasing of some of the basic Buddhist principles. I am inevitably subject to the Three Fires, subject to greedy desire to my advantage, to wild anger whenever my wishes are thwarted, and to basic ignorance out of which I deem myself over and above all that is. And this is the cause of our personal as well as of our very real present-day problems.

Thus the Buddhist teaching of Non-I (selflessness) would seem to be an effective antidote, as would the Zen Way of training, along which the Three Fires are extinguished by transforming their energy, and of bringing up the little selfish I to become a responsible and considerate human being, a good husbandman rather than a ravisher and exploiter, a good friend rather than a foe. All these possibilities are entirely within the field of nature, but they cannot be realised without effort exerted on oneself. We want to change and improve the situation, little expecting that we all made it and contribute to it.

To undo it, we have to change ourselves. When a cart is stuck in the mire, do you whip the cart or the ox?

The Buddhist principles reflect clear, unbiased observation of natural principles. The Zen Way removes the I-coloured spectacles. The shifts which occur along the way, and which are a restructuring of the total man, reintegrate him meaningfully into the world he and his nature are part of. Awareness of this makes him a conscious and responsible participator and husbandman. This restores his lost inheritance, the sense of awe and wonder of what is and what he is, which is much more than any I could ever dream of in the most exalted fantasies. There is nothing static in Life as it lives itself in its forms. Awakening brings to the individual the awareness of the dignity of being a conscious servant and agent in the processes of nature. Indeed, it is in such an awakened man that the processes of nature become conscious of themselves. Hence, in all that lives is built in a striving towards just that, a groping and yearning of nature which in man can find fulfilment.

With this in mind we can look again at the Buddhist formulation of the Wheel of Being (p. 12), which takes on a living meaning rather than appearing to be a quaint out-of-date doctrine. The Teaching becomes alive as we learn to 'see clearly'.

The shift is a natural process, a natural growing up that takes place when certain conditions are fulfilled. It is nothing 'unknown'; it is striven for by nature and it involves the total man.

What has gone wrong with us? Physically we must grow up; mentally, too, our intellects are schooled, hence our various systems of learning and education in general. Though there are individual cases of retarded growth, we note that physically retarded growth is less common than mentally retarded growth, or to put it another way, fewer dwarfs are born than mentally handicapped children. Emotionally, however, we seem collectively retarded, our development lop-sided.

Physically we are a long way removed from stone-age man in build and shape of head, body, limbs; mentally the difference is even greater, hence our disastrous impact on stone-age societies. But emotionally, we are hardly less irascible, greedy and frightened. Such lop-sided development puts us under considerable strain, the components growing ever wider apart, the split gaping more and more, with the result that nature makes convulsive attempts to bridge or heal it which render us enthusiastically gullible.

In the ordinary process of growing, shifts are normal phenomena of life, adaptations to new sets of circumstances. They occur even in some minerals; at a certain temperature and pressure the lattice structure becomes unstable and snaps over into what fits the present conditions. Quartz is an example. In the organic kingdom this ability makes growth and development possible. So we may see it as a response to circumstance as well as a factor of both growing up and development. Language shows the correlations, analogies we have culled from plant and animal; ripeness is maturity, being fully grown; growing further is evolution, line of development. The 'ripe', developed, fully grown, hence whole, individual contains the past, is the present, and points to and actually shapes the future, for it is in him as a nascent state. The Buddhist formulation of the law of Karma expresses the nature of this well, for it takes man's physical and psychological components as a unity. There seems to be an inherent drive towards individual wholeness for without it development cannot occur, or else becomes lop-sided and warped.

Real wholeness is therefore not rigidity but fluid adaptability. Behavioural scientists have studied facets of this ever since Pavlov trained his dogs by forcing them through emotional shifts. Though these do also occur when artificially forced they tend to short-circuit the natural process and arise prematurely, dislocating the container which has not had time to develop sufficient tensile strength to stand the shift.

Premature shifts are reversible, immature, and lead to instability which seriously disrupts and finally shatters the container. In man and animal over-forcing breaks the container and with that the spirit breaks.

Emotions are derivatives of instinctual energy and as such are capable of acting as natural guides if not interfered with by I A Mahayana (Northern Buddhist) expression of this is that the passions are the Buddha Nature and vice versa: inherently, that is, for in their manifestation they are poles apart, yet it is the same energy. Hence the futility of trying to cut off one's emotions. They are manifested life force. How could that be cut? And by whom? Who is the would-be cutter wanting to do what suits him? It is I, liable to be invaded by emotions and seeking to secure control.

There is reason for this. I am apt to lose control and may be swept into primitive behaviour by emotional eruptions, or be so carried away by them that I can no longer function or sustain directed and concentrated activity in such a state of possession. As there is a premium on efficient performance today as in the past, it may well be that man short-circuited his emotional development and integration, shoving it out of the way, as it were, and neglecting it rather than the slow and difficult task of transforming – 'bringing up' – the emotions. Naturally these have thus remained primitive, with the result that I feel a whole dimension missing; and, moreover, feel threatened and often overcome by this tremendous force in its primitive manifestation.

The Zen Way seeks to restore the balance by undertaking just this up-bringing of the emotional aspect. Before we can begin to consider how this can actually be brought about we have to look at another aspect of this shift; we have to look, so to speak, at the other end of the emotional scale.

Again, the passions are the Buddha nature and vice versa. Fundamentally they are the energy of life and like all energy must move between two poles, slide along gradients, to function. So far we have been concerned with the one pole, the physiological end, the wild primitivity. In Zen training, the transformation of this is likened to the taming and gentling of a splendid, tremendously strong, powerful, wild and quite ungovernable bull who stands for the compulsive, wild, primitive, stubborn aspect of emotional energy with which the heart is correlated, not for 'mind', however spelled. This again serves as a reminder that this crucial Buddhist term stands for 'heart' in all its connotations.

A digression here is in place. This training analogy has various formulations, either gentling the wild bull, or starting with a black bull which gradually becomes white, in eight or ten stages. The versions, accompanied by drawings, are available in English, usually translated as 'ox-herding' or even 'cow-herding pictures'.[7]

---

7. DT Suzuki, *Manual of Zen Buddhism* (Rider 1957); Tsujimuva and Tresor, tr., *The Ox and His Herdsman* (Hokuseido Press 1969). This is an excellent translation, but its real value is that it gives the comments on this text made by a contemporary Rinzai Zen master to his disciples.

Both 'ox' and 'cow' are unfortunate translations as the connotations do not express the quality inherent in the original term. Perhaps they were mistaken for the generic form of the species '*bos*' (Latin) which the English language lacks but which is used in the Chinese original and often appears in Zen texts.

So the 'heart-bull' is the wild, primitive aspect of the emotional force. The difficult task of the herdsman, man, is to gentle this wild bull by training, to 'bring him up', and to humanise his manifested energy. Thus the bull – 'searched for', 'found', 'gentled', 'carries the man', 'home', 'vanishes' – for he and the man have now become one. 'Deliverance from the Wheel of Being is only possible in the human state'.

A genuine transformation has taken place, the primitive wildness and compulsion hold sway no more, for they are changed. But this is not the end of the training analogy, and the pictorial presentation very clearly points both the Way and also the danger of what can go wrong at this point. For in the next picture, after the bull is 'brought up' on a par with man – hence 'bull vanished, man left' – the man also vanishes.

This approaches the other end of the emotional scale, obviously operative in man only, and here we have to be very careful because it is so easily confused with the primitive. In the mammal the differentiation does not (yet) exist. Its emergence from the physiological substratum and its gradual differentiation from it may be observed in the rites of primitive tribes, and in the picture-language of mythology where physiological analogues serve to point to the corresponding 'top end' of the scale for which expressions are lacking. In early agricultural communities it was often customary for the farmer to have sexual intercourse with his wife in the field to render it fertile. And mystics trying to express themselves tend to make use of the language of love.

Seemingly, this has been a bugbear and a continuous source of misunderstanding through the centuries. Such analogues are pointers forward, and since they have correspondences at the other end of the scale, they are uncannily accurate as pointers. Taking such pointers at their word level is not just short-sighted but leads back inevitably to the primitive pole; since this is now regression, the unleashed emotional energy turns destructive. Movements like antinomianism, or religious orgies, though they crop up again and again, are in themselves always shortlived. But in common with other religious formulations they show clearly man's difficulty in differentiating the two poles, and that when 'gripped', there is an almost irresistible gravity-pull back to the physiological end of the scale. Thus all developed religions stress some form of asceticism as part of their discipline, in order to make differentiation possible, and to disengage emotions from the physiological end.

Only if emotional energy is really 'humanised' can a valid differentiation be achieved. Actually, the one is the other. But with this manifests a new danger. Since the nature of energy is to move, to slide along gradients, if it can no longer go backward it is liable to crash forward, for it has lost none of its force in transformation. Indeed, it cannot be reduced at all. 'When used, it is inexhaustible', as the *Tao Te Ching* states.[8] Hence ripeness is all; if it can be contained, it cannot escape.

Today, there is much concern with 'experience', and in particular with what William James called 'religious experience'.

8. Ch'u Ta-Kao, tr., *Tao Te Ching* (Allen & Unwin 1970).

Rudolf Otto in his excellent little book *The Idea of the Holy*[9] is concerned with the upper end of the emotional scale; his term 'mysterium tremendum' aptly renders the numinosity of this 'mysterium' which is unknowable, hence a mystery; as blinding as brilliant light; tremendous, hence awe-inspiring; and totally overwhelming.

To adopt a temporary working model to help us with the differentiation we can say that emotional energy at the biological and physiological pole has the force of compulsion; at the upper, spiritual end of the pole, it is sheer numinosity which overwhelms.

In the bull-herding analogy, the man vanishes. This is the moment when the shift we are discussing occurs. If the container is not ready, if the shift is forced with little or no preparation, the container is dislocated and/or shattered. The balance is delicate. If the shift is striven for too hotly, too self-ishly, true ripening does not take place. Hence the Buddhist stress on 'right effort', on the 'Middle Way', on bowing, abdicating, true humility. There are innumerable warnings against striving outright for spiritual achievement; spiritual pride is a fetter that needs to be broken or the process is short-circuited and at best productive of a personality of remarkable but brute strength. The man is then very much there, in fact it could be said that he has become a bull-man.

This is what religious observances try to guard against. What they try to foster and further is a sense of devotion, a voluntary abdication before the numinous to prepare the approach to it.

9. Rudolf Otto, *The Idea of the Holy* (Oxford University Press, trans. JW Harvey, 1936).

Ideally, these are the outward expressions of an inner attitude, an attitude of the heart, and as such are the natural safeguards against becoming a bull-man. Hence the delicate balance mentioned above; hence the importance of bowing, laying oneself down again and again. Then the bow can grow and become a real service of joyful dedication in which the wonder of what is can suddenly and safely emerge. But such an attitude is not easily or naturally found these days. Effort and 'letting go' need to balance each other and cancel each other out.

In religious observances, too, there is a danger of over-shooting the balance, of over-zealousness. A story from India illustrates this. For years and years a man had been meditating in the forest, praying to Krishna for liberation. One day Krishna, having decided to bring it to him, approached him from behind and laid a hand upon his shoulder. 'How dare you disturb me, do you not see I am meditating?' the man burst out furiously. So Krishna went sadly away.

It is truly a razor-sharp path. Only a humble holding on to one's humanity in the face of the powers and dangers that assail us – the emotional energy – matures us truly.

Now we can again look at the stage in the bull-herding analogy where the man, too, vanishes. A new danger-point arises, for the man may be 'carried away' rather than be dissolved.

We have to refer back to the shift. As we now know, the container needs to be strong but flexible to hold and be restructured; if not, dislocation occurs. In the 'forward' end of the emotional scale, this dislocation is known as seizure. It is often mistaken for religious experience.

Ordinary language is a pointer to that mistake, for the term also has physical and pathological connotations. Whether physical or mental/psychological, it detracts from wholeness; it is more a symptom of possession and as such though it may even lead to the 'speaking with tongues', the possessed person is robbed of his integrity, swept out of the way and rendered an empty shell.

As a state, it is fortunately usually reversible, though inevitably one-sided. It invariably occurs at emotional 'highs', and is at best a cathartic experience to be remembered all one's life; it may carry a man away for good, or invade him temporarily.

As a phenomenon it is well known and attested; as an affliction it is virulent and infectious. In its religious form it thrives on mass movements such as revivalist meetings and the modern equivalents. Pop 'culture' is akin to it, as its preoccupation with psychedelics shows, and its roots on the most primitive scale are in the phenomenon of 'running amok'.

In the individual, religious seizure may be induced by over-zealousness or impatience, forced by excess of fasting, high altitude and isolation. We are in well-known territory, though on a somewhat higher rung of the emotional scale. The mechanism, however, is the same. The 'lower end' belongs more to the physiological pole, hence the mass aspect. The closer individuality is approximated, the more it changes attitude from one extreme to the other, with compulsion still clinging to it, more often than not as fanaticism.

The question is, how did 'seizure' become associated with the stage of 'man vanished too'? Rudolf Otto says of the 'mysterium tremendum' that its impact has the power to 'deeply and profoundly move', which is something very different from being cleanly carried away. In the latter, no merging can occur, no coming together is possible; there is no confrontation, and seeing cannot take place. But in the former the structure holds because it is flexible enough to take the terrific impact which produces the shift without disruption and from which interaction a new, all-inclusive, all-embracing totality arises. This is no overstatement, for to the impact of the 'absolutely other' belongs a quality of ghostly other-worldliness that makes the flesh creep, the hair stand on end and turns the heart round. The experience of it is total and the physical component belongs to it as much as the inner or psychological one.

The phrase 'awe and wonder' is well chosen for it. To tie it up with the bull-herding analogy, the bull, vanished, has become the numinosity – the passions are the Buddha Nature when gentled and transformed.

If such an experience befalls a man who is at least reasonably prepared, one might also say humble enough, the numinosity will render itself perceptible in the pictures of his religious values. If religious values are no longer 'true' for him, the experience of the impact will take on archetypal features in the Jungian sense, that is, configurations of what is grave and constant in human experience, but in individual imagery. Whatever the image or nature of manifestation, the quality of other-worldliness, ghostly and quite impersonal, always clings to it without being subject to reason or intellectual understanding, but overwhelmingly and utterly convincing.

Like the distant rumblings of an approaching storm, such 'experiences' are likely to occur at every stage – right from the beginning, all along the emotional scale, commanding instant recognition and obedience.

It is important therefore for the container to have the strength to hold its own against the images, that is not to identify without being swallowed by them, and yet be flexible enough to shift into the new attitude, now more adapted for 'renewal'.

There is a Zen saying, particularly apt for Japan which has many evergreen trees, that the old leaves are kind; they stay on to protect the buds forming underneath, but fall off when the buds are ready to come out. These experiences along the way also prepare for the decisive shift. This is the point where the way can go wrong, or rather not the way but the man.

If the man is carried away by such an experience, if he takes its 'pictures' as objective and final, he clings to these pictures with the deep conviction that belongs to the impact rather than the picture; he is thus stuck to the pictures and further growth is stultified, or cannot occur at all. Hence the warning against fashioning graven images.

A quality of finality does, indeed, cling to each experience of this type, for it constitutes a valid adaptation or new attitude. Hence the tremendous importance of the man enduring the impact, and his true humility, which is forged along the way of training, is essential. It is a question of 'suffering it out' again and again until the sufferer, I, is at last ready to fall off. A little of him dies every time and this makes the shift into a new attitude possible.

But what if such an experience happens when 'the man' is not there either? When the 'picture maker' is absent? Absent, not because he has been carried away prematurely and thus, though away, still *is*, but because *he* is nothing? Or, in the Buddhist analogy, when the wave has become aware of being ocean?

The bull-herding analogy calls that state 'into the origin, back to the source'. It could not be better expressed, for this is the true oneness, totality, and no separate I can see/experience THAT. Oneness and I are mutually exclusive. Of course, 'the man' must have 'gone'. This is also the place where what Master Hakuin terms the 'Great Death' has occurred: 'Great' because it is dying in and to Life, and Death because it is the death of I as I know it, and with that the end of fear including that of 'natural death'. The final shift has occurred, the restructuring has taken place; there is only life, the heart is liberated from the bonds of I; and with that its inherent warmth can flow freely and in full awareness.

With I, the man, dissolved 'at the origin, back to the source', there is a breaking into the non-personal realm of the creative spirit which now takes truly human shape and stature. This new, true man indeed cannot turn away; where should he go? He 'comes back to the market with bliss-bestowing hands', and takes up life as a full human being, reintegrated, restructured, consciously aware of what he is, and the humble servant of what he is. His front gate is firmly closed, neither Buddha nor Mara can find him who is not there, who is 'nothing'. With No I (*anatta*) there is no *volitional intention*, no interference, however well meant. Such a man leaves no trace, has sprung out of the karmic law; however, as a Zen story illustrates,[10] he does 'not obscure it' either. He works with it, is not beyond it. And so, he is neither bound by morals nor beyond them, for he has broken into the place from which all morality arises, and is genuinely and naturally 'good', that is both loving and wise. This also means that he is not blind; that he sees differences

10. Mumonkan, *Case 2: Hyakujo's Fox*

very clearly and distinguishes between Buddha and Mara, good and evil, recognising them when he sees them, they no longer have power over him, they cannot carry him away. Thus he is naturally 'good'.

Neither a saint not a sage, as such, but a human being, fully and totally so; and humbly human because aware of the human follies and the human miseries that beset us all. How could he understand others were he not? That is why he is wise. No longer the plaything of human follies. How could he help others, show them the way out, were he not? Master Hakuin therefore says of him that 'the nose is still vertical and the mouth horizontal' – that is, he happens to have a distinct body with the distinct features of such a body, and the tastes that go with it. In no way is he 'beyond' it – he will still prefer tea rather than coffee, for example, but the bottom will not fall out of his universe should there be no tea forthcoming.

As a total human being, restructured by suffering through the terrific impact of the 'mysterium tremendum', the final shift having taken place, all the ghostly, other-world numinosity of the 'totally other' has also become human in him, truly human.

There are echoes of this in Christianity too: 'Before Abraham was, I am', the son of man, and God having become man in 'the second person' of the trinity. Since no I can conceive of such things they have always been regarded as religious mystery. But the mystics of all ages speak the same language, for they have seen into this realm, and so speak 'as one'. To I, miracles need to correspond to my sense of mystery. But in the fullness which is beyond I the miraculous pervades what is. 'How wonderful, how miraculous, I carry wood and fetch water', as a Zen Master expressed it.

The total man working with what is, being one with it and in no way obscuring it or interfering with it, is not a worker of miracles like walking on the water or raising people from the dead. He knows nothing of death, but much of life, of its joys and sorrows, its beauty and ugliness. Though he can, and does, work 'miracles', they are entirely human; his heart is open, his total love and compassion soften sorrow and ugliness at a touch; his bliss-bestowing hands lift up his fellow beings, and less by words than by being what and as he is, he points the Way for those who wish to tread it – that Way of which the Buddha said that he had rediscovered it, an ancient way that leads to an ancient city. This is the Way of the Heart, as old as man, which can be walked by all who are so inclined. It is always available and leads to that ancient city, the full human Heart, which is also the Buddha Heart.

So when the Zen School calls itself the Buddha Heart School, in its very name it points the Way. It has transmitted it in a living chain and thus kept alive the lore of the way, the hardships, dangers and obstacles; but also the stages and the fullness of the Heart when it is finally reached.

APPLICATION

At this stage a re-reading of the chapter on the Buddha's life (p. 19) will help bring into relief the various points that have been made so far. Following the life of a monk through his noviciate in a temple and then through the training monastery (p. 43) highlights the same facets. Now we must ask ourselves what can we, here and now, do? With no temples or training monasteries, can anything be done at all? Surely the answer is 'Yes' – if we are so minded.

Though the monk's life is harder than ours, once he is settled in, it soon becomes routine, interrupted, as every routine is, by emotional flare-ups, resistances against 'what does not suit me'. The monk under discipline has little option; he cannot give in to or be carried away by such flare-ups; he has to take it as it comes, endure what arises in him while performing his daily work, whether he finds it easy or not. Whether this is merely soul-grinding, or whether it serves him as good practice to grind himself out, depends on him, on his own attitude.

We can decide to live our life in such an attitude. We can use the routine of our daily round as our training discipline, courageously facing emotional upheavals as and when they arise and enduring them willingly. Suffering them out again and again, we are following the footsteps of the Buddha.

How does this look in actual practice? Most of us have some kind of daily routine: a job to go to, housework to do, or a combination of both. But within this, we are quite free. A good deal is left to our own choice; if not what we do, then certainly when we do it. We can often shift around as it suits us, rather than do this now and that later – or vice versa. Our hours of rising or going to bed are fairly optional. But since we can never have everything exactly as it suits us this, too, raises problems. Worse, the more spoilt we are in this way, the more the smallest denial upsets us. So we are really not better off, though we naturally, but mistakenly, think that 'all is going well', as it suits us, we should be happy ever after, fulfilled, in fact! Since this, naturally, can never be, one should try a reversal of attitude, almost as a counter-irritant. I only want what suits me and get wildly upset if things run counter to that; if I just for a while would stop my wild pursuit of things, as it suits me, stop trying to manipulate things and just ponder, I must see that I can never have only what suits me. So my pursuit of what suits me is really point-less, a waste of effort and frustrating. Further clear thinking will make me aware that if it is impossible to have things always as they suit me, then the trouble is not with things but with I. I is overweening in its wants and appetites which, though validly there, are misinterpreted by me as I picture them. Thus the whole business of I and what I want becomes suspect. This helps the shift of attitude, and instead of the pursuit of external things, we become concerned with the trouble-maker I.

One can therefore try to follow the footsteps of the Buddha and to adopt his Way which leads out of this tangle of I and emo-tions. For how long? We could decide to take our daily life just as it is, as our training discipline, initially for three months only, or it might soon feel like an eternity and be forgotten like New Year's resolutions. We do not need to concoct anything special, just our ordinary daily routine, but fixing our times for getting up and going to bed. It is imperative to live that routine as it is, not shifting anything around as it suits me, or seems better to me, or more efficient, or even better practice; just to leave it alone and do what is to be done as best one is able. Thus, tied down, with so much of our usual freedom of shifting around curtailed, emotional reactions against that framework of discipline are inevitable and natural. This is part of the discipline, to act as a kind of tethering pole, and to teach us to function smoothly under circumstances of restriction of choice, of what I feel to be adverse circumstances.

Another purpose of such discipline is that in and through it we learn to recognise, accept, bear with, suffer out, our emotional tantrums, neither letting them rip nor repressing them. We adopt a willing attitude, in fact. This cannot be stressed too much and is very difficult to understand.

Both aspects of the discipline are closely connected and are in fact only two sides of the same thing, like two sides of a coin. The latter, suffering through emotional upsets, produces the former, the ability to function smoothly under all conditions. That this is the opposite of how we usually learn to function smoothly hardly needs to be stressed. How did it originate and why?

There is a premium on smooth performance, not only today in our complicated technological age, but of old where survival depended on it even more. Since the days when our ancestors hunted mammoth and bison, whether they were in the mood to do so or not, smooth performance and cooperation have been imperative. Since man is very much subject to his emotions, helpful means and rites to put him into the right mood have been developed from earliest times: hunting war dances, ploughing or sowing songs and close bonds of kinship to further cooperation. In all this, the stress is on performance, on how to overcome emotional hindrances, but not on the hindrance itself, the agent that is the spanner in the works.

We have all learned in the course of our upbringing and education how to suppress or repress our emotions for the sake of smooth and sustained performance. Having a little more free will at our disposal than our stone-age ancestors or present-day primitives, we can dispense with war and work-songs – though this is more apparent than real as today we have propaganda to get us into the mood. Today, in our more permissive, affluent society, we seem to have returned full circle to the emotional problems. They have never changed and have always held sway. The Western I especially wants to control them, or cut them off, not realising that they are not the property of any I, and are compelling I more often than not. It is the emotion that has me. Were it really mine, it would be subject to my will. I could produce it at will, and I could lay it down calmly – but in fact, I cannot do so.

I and emotions are both enemies and brothers-in-arms. I also have long learned my own way of shying away from emotions, of screening myself from their onslaught, in order to be able to function. But this does not lessen my problems.

With this discipline we start working from the other side. It is extremely hard. It is something which we have never done before, nor even known of; as a matter of fact it is just what we have studiously avoided and if we are willing to undertake such a training now, it is usually also from the motive of continuing to avoid it. Thus the actual discipline comes as a shock and is the opposite of what we expected. A thousand years ago Master Rinzai said that the ordinary person does not naturally take to it.

Experience has shown that it is extremely difficult to explain how to start such a practice or discipline. We have nothing in our experience or our cultural background to prepare us for it, not even any conceptual approximations. And everything we know, and indeed want, points the opposite way. I am used to taking control, want to manipulate everybody as they ought to be: in short, I need a picture as a frame of reference to work towards. It is therefore not surprising that I cannot take in what is outside my conceptual framework, and so am bound to follow the existing pattern without even realising it. Thus, only after trying for some time, and establishing a few concrete and experiential data is it possible to head I off the familiar track and to shift little by little on to the new one. Whatever we may think or believe we learn only by experience and becoming familiar with the 'new' pattern, establishing it only by actually doing it. As in riding a bicycle, or playing the piano, or learning to write, or learning a language, the process consists of constant repetition until we are used to it.

Why should this be so difficult to see and accept? Do we ever ask ourselves what the words we use so glibly when it suits us actually mean or what they point to? What is inconceivable or unimaginable, is surely just what we cannot imagine or conceive; it is totally other, quite outside our frame of reference. If it attracts us we naturally speculate about it but can bring nothing to it but our existing conceptions, based as they are on our concrete experiences. These we may then combine in strange, abstract patterns like a woman's head on a lion's body, or a man's body with an elephant's head, arbitrarily combining what actually is separate. If I have neither seen a cat nor a picture of one, what image will I form in my mind if you – however accurately – describe or explain one to me? The whole cat, rather than only what may intrigue you in a cat, or what you have seen of it, the tail and the whiskers, or the vanishing grin? Can one explain or describe colour to a man born blind? If I see blue, it is only because my eyes perceive a certain wavelength of light as blue; and if I happen to be colour-blind my eyes will perceive and interpret a certain wavelength as green which you will see as red.

We are lazy. We rarely bother to really think things through, or else we shy away from doing so because the result might be uncomfortable. Yet this is the proper province of our thinking faculty, rather than letting it disport itself in the region of feelings and emotions where it is naturally 'blind'.

How can one describe what the icy snow peaks look like to a man who has never left the equatorial jungle, has seen no pictures of them and does not even have a telly? He has no conception of them. Listening to a description, his imagination works: white – but what does he know of the dazzling white of virgin snow sparkling in bright sunshine if he has never been out of the green shade of the forest? The exhilarating air, the icy cold – but the more he is told, the more his imagination conjures up pictures known to him, combines them; and the more he is deluded by the picture he has formed and now believes.

I do not really accept this fact. A little sober thinking is helpful. How do we picture 'heaven', 'hell', 'God', the 'devil'? As blacker or more brilliant, uglier, more beautiful, more fearful than we concretely know, but in no way out of our factual experience. Incidentally, this is why we tend to have trouble when we move out of our cultural background where such attributes are conventionally fixed. A ghost may carry his head, or skull, under the arm, he may clank about dragging chains but he does walk, clop-clop or slurp-slurp. His Japanese equivalent has, surprise, no feet at all. We would never have thought it, would we? It would not have occurred to us in our wildest imaginings. But when we are told, we can take it because we also have ghosts and feet are not unfamiliar to us.

And the wholly other? How do we behave with that? Even if a spiritualist medium speaking in the voice of my dead aunt Mary, describes her present whereabouts they are never totally other. The flowers may be brighter, the grass greener, the world happier, the beings more ethereal – a difference of intensity which serves to suggest the intended otherness, but is not really 'other'. On the other side of the imaginative spectrum of 'other-ness', science fiction has the greatest difficulty in portraying the otherness of beings on other planets; in most cases they turn out to be either like man or like animals with intelligence; a few of the most imaginative combine again into weird conglomer-ates, but nothing is wholly other as one might actually expect it to be on a planet quite different from ours. We can be sure that if portrayal of the wholly other were possible, our science fiction writers would have hit upon it.

I am slow to take in what I do not particularly fancy, what might detract from my self-esteem. Such a consideration is actually frightening and I would rather avoid it.

There is only one thing that can render conceivable what is really unknown, namely one's own experience of it. As Master Hakuin suggested, a man wishing to know how sea water tastes wastes his time speculating about it; he needs to start walking and keep walking straight on till he comes to the sea (the country he is referring to is Japan, an island). As he stoops to dip his finger into it, and licks off the drops, he knows at that instant the taste of all the seven oceans.

The first shock that comes to an I wanting to start on the Zen Way is the realisation that I cannot understand it. And if I want to do it, I need to take it on trust – the Great Root of Faith. And as I start, I need to check and recheck every step to avoid falling back into long-established habit patterns without even being aware of having done so – the Great Root of Doubt. And since this Way leads to what I have always avoided, and indeed wish to avoid for good, it needs Passionate, almost desperate Strength to face and endure.

These are the three traditional requisites. But since a 20th-century Western I is a very stiff-necked, arrogant, impatient, acquisitive fellow, two more requisites can be usefully added: Great Patience and Great Humility.

The Zen Way, and Buddhism, are not native to our culture. The recent interest in things Eastern has resulted in a great number of books about them, and translations of their scriptures but, however bilingual one may be, how can one translate a subject one does not know? Thus most books already carry a slant, and even translations are not necessarily correct as to meaning and less so as to connotations. Nor can they really convey what is alien, other, to our way of thinking. Some warping at least is inevitable. Our interest is stirred by those books which we then use as points of reference for our own picture-making. If the picture is, so to speak, alluring enough it may incite us to start a practice, in order to possess ourselves of that picture from which we hope 'salvation', the solution to all our troubles and tribulations. I want to be all the delectable things, such as liberated, free, mindful and self-possessed, and of course enlightened, which I interpret entirely personally, according to my lights and so am quite willing to go in pursuit of them.

Then the practice starts totally different from what I expected and was led to believe. This is not what I came here for – which in a way is perfectly true. The more I cling to my lovely pictures, the weaker I really am. Clinging to them as for life, I cannot let go of them, and so stop and give up practice.

If I am humble enough to accept the reversal, the dethronement of my pictures, and patient enough to give the practice at least a try, unexpected things begin to emerge. If I decide to live my daily life with its daily routine just as it is, to accept what comes at the time and do it as best I can, problems arise at once. I naturally see this as accepting circumstances, situations, requests, as the objective. But this is not very important, for in the routine of our jobs and work we have to do it anyway. Besides, objects are not mine, and I will never have control over them. But my reactions are mine. What I have to accept and become familiar with are my emotional reactions, my resistances, when something happens which does not suit me. Those reactions are truly mine, though I do not like them and have long trained myself to turn a blind eye towards my little reactions. Yet these are both the disturbers and the obstacles.

Familiarity with the workings of the emotional household is the first step in the training. To begin with, I inevitably feel myself to be the agent: '*I* accept *this*'; we are back at the subject-object split; the practice goes wrong or gives me a swollen head. For when I try to appropriate the emotional energy, the practice soon gets both boring and bothersome. I give it up.

How does one 'accept' one's own emotional resistances and reactions? Not by disowning them, nor by refusing to see them, for it is just that which gives them power over us; hence the need for reversal.

If we are sitting cosily together and you ask me to make a cup of tea, if I want one myself I will trot off happily to make it. But if I am sitting engrossed in a book which fascinates me, or am doing something I deem important, then such a request is apt to evoke a resistance: 'drat it', or 'always just at this moment', I am angry at being disturbed, and therefore exasperated by your lack of consideration: 'can't he/she see ... ', or at the least I am tempted to snap out: 'for once, make it yourself'. If I am carried away to say so, I would then have to accept that once again, for the umpteenth time, I had failed in my practice, had let the emotions carry me away. No blame attaches to the other – it is *my* reaction.

But if I am serious with my practice I may at least manage to keep my mouth shut despite being sorely tempted otherwise. And after the initial impact of the flare-up is over, I may consider that my practice is first to accept the emotional reaction and then the request. So I bestir myself to go and make the tea. The first round is won. But it may immediately go wrong, for on my way to put the kettle on I may begin to congratulate myself on how good I am to do so in spite of having been disturbed, and how much progress I seem to be making with my practice. This is I trying to appropriate the act in order to feel good – particularly because now I do not wish to see what is actually going on inside myself. For if I can refrain from congratulating myself and have the courage and honesty to look at what is actually going on inside me at that moment, I will have to acknowledge that I can barely make myself go because I am so angry. So I accept this anger *and* make that tea, fully aware of my boiling emotion. This is the difficulty, to learn to do what is really foreign to us; to be open to our emotional affects *and* to function smoothly.

Since we suffer from emotional onslaughts, we need to learn to bear them and suffer them willingly in full awareness. Does that remind us of the Buddha's teaching: 'Suffering I teach, and the Way out of Suffering'? We must not turn our back on what goes on inside us for the sake of good performance, but learn to perform in the state of suffering.

An emotional reaction is energy rising up, compelling action, hence in the human state, blind, because unconscious. For example, in hitting out physically or verbally, energy flows into the action and we are thus relieved of tension. If this escape is not allowed, it is apt to turn in on us and lames our performance. We shrivel up internally and are more or less incapacitated.

The more we give in to one or the other, the more our tolerance decreases, and the more we become the shuttlecock of our emotions. Too much permissiveness, too much release, though temporarily relaxing tension, make things worse rather than better in the long run. As we know, repressing the emotions is not the answer either, for sooner or later they erupt violently or invade us unaware.

Though I shy away from this double burden of functioning smoothly in spite of being in a state of emotional agitation, yet precisely this 'suffering in action' is the transforming agent. It deals with the cause rather than with the symptom of our affliction. However, this suffering is not something that I can actively do – I watching myself – it is a passive but willing, patient, dumb endurance; a being open to the impact of the emotions and letting them grate and grind inside. The active part of I is not concerned with this process but only with the effort to continue functioning smoothly in spite of it, though remaining fully aware of it. This is what real acceptance training is about. No I can do it from the word go. It needs much practice, much trial and error, before it is really understood.

I also tend to get despondent on finding out that not only is this practice difficult, but that I fail more often than not in it. But this is only natural. If I could do it from the very start, as I naïvely expect when I make up my mind to do it, there would be no need for such practice.

Meanwhile, I learn a lot from realising that I cannot do the practice by an act of will, which sobers my self-esteem; moreover, with no object to blame, I begin to suspect that actually I am my own obstacle. If all goes well this is the first little shift, the first softening up of the rigid I. With it the danger arises of I latching on to it, of I beginning to analyse myself, trying to catch myself – which leads to nothing, only reflection upon reflection like in a hall of mirrors with no end to it. 'The eye that sees but cannot see itself; the sword that cuts but cannot cut itself.' Indeed, the Great Doubt is essential all the way and a guide is important to point out the Way yet again whenever I quite unbeknown to myself have once more taken over in all good faith.

I cannot deal with my emotional upheavals; I can only suffer them out. By neither letting the emotional energy escape into blind reaction, nor letting it lame me and hinder my action, but holding and bearing it, my tolerance develops rather as physical training develops muscle strength and stamina. That means I can tolerate more emotional energy and the container grows stronger. Since there is also less resistance, it is usually experienced as an influx of energy. This is another danger-point to watch out for – I like to feel stronger. And this is where a religious practice like the Zen Way is so helpful with its stress on bowing: I-abdication. In the grip of an emotional onslaught, bowing can be extremely helpful just because in the mere physical action, not necessarily I, but the rest of me understands and is more ready to give in. Out of this develops the flexibility that must accompany strength.

The difficulty is that I invariably misunderstand the bowing and giving in. From the standpoint of I, it means giving in to the object, being on a par with it. Since the object is other than I this means loss of integrity. Yet, the purpose of the exercise is not to get caught up with the object, but simply to learn to give in. The 'wilful will' experienced as 'I must...' needs gentling. Religions facilitate this by directing the giving in to a 'higher authority'; whether this be conceived anthropomorphically or as a neutral law, it is other than and above both subject and object. A good bit of my reasonable uneasiness with regard to this giving in vanishes if it is seen as giving in to something more than I, and other than the object; with that, the object becomes less important. Such giving in does not rob me of my integrity but actually enhances it.

It is always a two-way process and both I and the emotional energy change by this interaction. As a temporary working model (cf. p. 91), think of I as a spiky ball, each spike being one of my habitual reactions: 'I want', 'I must', 'I can't', 'I won't', 'I am right'. These spikes hurt the ball, me, like thorns in my living flesh, as they draw up emotional energy and charge the ball. If the energy is neither discharged (blame of object, and consequent action) nor allowed to hinder my functioning, it just sparks and/or boils inside me. Movement is its function and so it does the conducive work of acting in me as motor-energy, grinding those spikes away, little by little. Being life-energy, it is the only thing strong enough to do so.

Hence the importance of it being contained – rather than allowed to flare up and discharge itself like lightning, or to lame and cripple performance. In doing this conducive work, which it alone can do, the energy exhausts its potential in the work of grinding the spikes down and in so doing both itself and I change. This interaction is essential for any valid change which is more than a momentary 'high', inevitably followed by its corresponding 'low'.

In the bull-herding analogy, this is the interaction between man and bull, the taming of the bull. The bull is so hard to find because he is so totally unexpected. He is not somewhere outside, not in the teachings or scriptural lore; nothing to do with me either – just the emotional reactions when they flare up. Truly this is the last place one would expect to find that magnificent bull.

This then is how to start the practice. Another unexpected, and frightening, aspect, especially to a rigid I, is that at the beginning I seem to become more emotional, and worse rather than better. If this is the case then enough 'right effort' has gone into the practice; the blinkers are off, and I no longer turn a blind eye to the many little frustrations and annoyances that also make up my daily life. They have, in fact, always been there, but I had not been aware of them; only the bigger ones have been strong enough to make me aware of their impact and to carry me away with their force. Those bigger ones do not constitute our training ground; they are too strong. Our concern is with the little ones; as soon as they emerge and as we become familiar with them, they are the helpmates in our practice. We just manage to hold and endure them.

Hence the importance of being aware of them. An I heavily resisting the emotions and thus habitually repressing them, is quite convinced of not having any emotional difficulties, and is in consequence rather vacuous, only half alive. Or I have become a compulsive doer, restlessly kept busy by the emotions now forcing their discharge through action. Their charge then lends grave importance to the most trivial things, even creating 'tasks' which in themselves are nothing but lead their victim ever more away from actual daily life, its activity, relationships, and warmth.

The first step then is cautiously to work on the practice and, little by little, to uncover the emotional household. Nothing can be done without first becoming aware of and then familiar with it. The bull must first be found, then caught, before the job of training and gentling him can begin. The strength and magnificence of the bull should now be fairly clear. And it seems reasonable that before setting out to catch and tame him we might pause for a moment to take stock, to see where our feet really stand and whether they stand on fairly firm ground. If we are slipshod, the bull will certainly run away with us, should we stumble across him.

Emotional energy is life-force, the full strength and magnificence of the bull, even in his wild, primitive aspect. From the very start, it is better that our attitude vis-a-vis the bull should be one of awe and wonder, not one of enmity. Though he is wild, he is what we are after. This attitude is essential for the gentling and taming once we have found him.

Of course, the bull is stronger than I. Of course, he is wild from of old. Of course, he does not want to give up his wayward habits and if I really want to tame him, I am in for a troublesome time. If I use brute force, he will turn at once against me and win every bout. So my attitude in the training must be that of sustained perseverance which, in the long run, will wear him out; hanging onto him as well as I can, even if he drags me. Thus

I become familiar with the bull and he with me. Struggling with each other we learn to tolerate each other and to understand each other. We both change in the process.

Initially it is important only to be concerned with the little emotional flurries in ordinary daily life and to learn the willing endurance while functioning smoothly. If we are sincere we are always inclined to take more upon ourselves than we can actually carry over a long period. I may be able to drag a heavy suitcase to the top of the road but I cannot manage to lug it all the way to the station.

Usually we do not like to concern ourselves only with what is small. It is worthwhile finding out why not. We equate small with bothersome. Why? And who is the judge of what is small or great? Something stirs at the word great; it catches our interest; we respond to it, feel we have a share in it. It is a pole to which emotional energy flows, hence a natural striving. But I, deluded and short-sighted (one of the three Signs of Being), am not a good judge. Have we ever inquired what standard or yardstick we use for our *ex cathedra* judgements, and on what assumptions they are based? My lofty standards are fired from underneath by emotions, and since I am and/or keep myself unaware of this, they are of a very selfish nature.

A Zen teacher said of his disciples that from time to time they would try to make an effort to do some 'Great Good' thing for him, unselfishly. He would notice the signs in the abstraction in their eyes, and their forgetfulness in their everyday tasks. Conditions would become difficult and when all were beginning to suffer from them, he would ask them to return to normal, just doing their usual tasks as well as possible; nothing he said would please him more, or be more conducive for them all.

There is a lesson here which deserves long and careful pondering. If I *try* to be too unselfish, too good, or attempt to do something too great, there is more greed behind it than in the ordinary natural selfishness, and it automatically brings up the opposite; hence things go wrong. We know this but from time to time we are still 'fired' and carried away.

Whether we like it or not we live in a bipolar world; all the opposites are contained in it, the 10,000 things, as the Chinese express it. And we are part of this world. The more we resist or refuse one part, the more power we give it. The whole world wants peace, and violences increases. A big tree has deep roots and strong light casts dark shadows.

Our world is fundamentally just as it is. Its inherent natural laws have shaped it and the life it has brought forth. For better or worse, we have changed it enormously. But we have not conquered nature because we can ride in the sky, or split the atom; we have merely learned to understand some of nature's laws and use them as it suits us. Our times show that we are not good, intelligent, or unselfish users.

The fault is not with the world, but with us – with you and me. And so we must look to ourselves rather than outside if we want to do something about it. This brings us back to the Buddha's Way, to ourselves walking it diligently, rather than being dazzled and misled by great words.

Using our daily life as our training discipline, functioning in it whilst holding ourselves open to all emotional impacts and willingly enduring their grating and grinding, with open eyes, we begin to change.

The world has its inherent laws that have shaped it, and brought forth what is. These laws are tremendously great, miraculous and good in their context. They include the faculty of change – evolving. From nebula to globe, from organic sludge to us – and all that only a speck in a remote corner of the universe. Our mind reels, it is so stupendous, and so utterly humbling. Yet we have a place in it, equally tremendous; if I become what I am, no-thing, then the heart-mirror is clear and truly reflects what is. With that, the process of becoming, and of being, has awakened, has become conscious, and reflects itself. This is the position and responsibility of the human state, from which alone further development is possible. Do we live up to it? Individually and collectively?

So we knuckle under and continue the training. And come to the stage where we are now seriously grappling with the bull.

Why does the notion of anything great stir us? Our longing goes out towards it. But why? Is it not that usually we do not feel we are living our life fully, that something more, something greater is ahead, beckoning? The pettiness of our daily life makes us yearn even more for something great to happen, something great enough to take us out of ourselves. These phrases are revealing. When confronted with something great, or with a sudden great problem, we react quite differently from our usual habit. It seems as if the great brings forth the whole of us and so our reaction is a total one. The total reaction and total effort is what we are now concerned with in our practice. It takes practice, training, to be able to do it, for surprisingly, conscious total effort is both a matter of fearlessness and of obedience; a response to circumstance, or, to express it neutrally, to the scheme of things. In itself, it is natural – a child reacts in this way, unstintingly, giving itself to what it is doing. If the tiny hand grips, it grips totally, nothing is held back, deliberated, saved. Total effort is all out – not I doing, but I giving myself completely. Hence the matter of obedience. That means again the Middle Way, neither I self-consciously wanting or trying to bring forth the total effort; that always falls short, my very intention being the obstacle. Nor is it an impulsive giving in and being carried away; though the totality is in it, it is blind.

The Dutch sailing proverb quoted earlier expresses this two-way function ('God helps the sailor, but he must steer himself'). This is required of us. In an emergency, if something great occurs, it is an almost automatic response that I *whole-heartedly,* unstintingly, go all out and completely give myself to what I am doing. I lose myself in it. Now I have to learn to do this in full awareness. It seems that this activates 'the other side' which then can and does respond.

And if not? Well, one can only do one's utmost, whole-heartedly, and without clinging to a result. Sometimes one wins, sometimes one loses. What is important is the total effort. The surprising thing is that the whole-heartedness makes the event subjectively great to me, even if I lose. I have wholly, fully, lived it, and so it has meaning. As in a game it was fair play and good sport. Today, we have all but forgotten such things.

If I judge something as small, I react accordingly and so only act half-heartedly, only half there. My response is sluggish or hesitating, for to me it seems little and meaningless. Continuing such a course my life becomes increasingly shallow, meaningless, drifting through trivia. I long for some great event to which I can respond heroically and which consequently will make me, the 'no-thing', into 'some-thing'. This is the fallacy of I.

If I could only refrain from judging and whole-heartedly embrace what comes, and respond wholly, fully, to everything – and this is what the Acceptance Practice in Daily Life has begun to teach me – then my longing for the great would begin to wane; the truly great is contained in the total act and effort. Life is lived fully; thus the feeling of being vitally alive, the zest and joy that go with it. Life lived wholly acquires meaning and purpose; it is brimful of wonder at what is and of awe at the mystery to which the heart inclines as to its real home.

Thus 'right effort' is a self-forgetting. This is not easily come by, and approaching it, we meet fear.

We have already seen that the very nature of I is fear. Now we begin to meet this naked fear, and it is a very difficult stage in the practice. To me it seems fraught with danger to go unstintingly into total effort which, moreover, is not mine but rather a forgetting of myself without losing awareness – the opposite of an impulsive response. Hence the fear, for I am neglected: I who always want to do, to act, to manipulate, to plan, and above all need to be in control. But there is reason for that fear and it must not be approached lightly or without adequate preparation. I am terrified of losing myself.

At this stage the fear is of losing oneself, and this lends it that special flavour of panicky terror and resistance. That fear tries, and can, prevent the all-out effort required, and it is bound to do so if in the beginning the practice was not thorough enough. Here, too, the gesture of abdication, of bowing, is of great help. Only I can be afraid!

So, little by little, as life becomes more meaningful and as trust begins to develop, I lose some of my importance, and to that extent, the root of fear can be approached safely. It seems as if I, afraid of fear, run after objects to distract myself. In the training, as I learn to give in, as the bull becomes tamer and gentler, this fear seems to come closer. In fact, it was always there, but I hid myself from it, covered it up under layers of objects. In the practice, as the objects begin to drop off, the veil becomes thinner, till I, softened, can bear the proximity of fear, and finally look it in the face. At this moment both I and fear vanish. A turning over in depth has taken place, leaving only reflecting awareness.

The practice in daily life is not easy. Experience has shown that without actually having tried it for a few weeks, and thus having some concrete experience of it, the acceptance is inevitably directed to the object which is all I know and wish to overcome, to conquer. But true acceptance needs to be directed to my emotional reactions. What makes me react emotionally, the object, is not mine and I have no influence over it; but as long as there is I, I am bound to react. This is the being bound on the Wheel.

What is undoubtedly mine is the reaction and that is a cause that can be worked out by means of total effort. Whenever one is invaded by such a reaction, one accepts its impact, bearing it willingly and dumbly but in full awareness, not refusing the suffering nor closing one's eyes against it.

In Buddhist terms, I, we all, seem to be bound upon the Wheel of Being, shuttling willy-nilly through the Six Paths, suffering helplessly with no redress, with eyes closed, trying not to take it in, trying not to see. This is *Samsara,* the world of suffering and dissatisfaction; avoiding as much as we can, and wearing ourselves out with it, a self-perpetuating process.

The Buddha, the Awakened One, told us: 'Suffering I teach, and the Way out of Suffering.' This Way out is not one of avoidance, nor of escape. We know that he faced his suffering and the problems that confronted him and that he suffered them out and came through them.

Following his footsteps does not mean imitating him. It means facing our own problems, our emotional onslaughts, as courageously and willingly as he did his, with open eyes. Seeing and learning from them in the process, we go right through them, through the middle of the sea of suffering – perhaps the most profound connotation of the 'Middle Way' when all suffering is suffered out, there is an end of it. This is the coming out on the other side, on the other shore, Nirvana.

Willingly suffering it out, not resisting, not turning away, in full 'meek' awareness, this is the difficulty. It is a very delicate balance which I can easily disturb. Again, the Buddha is our guide: neither too much austerity, which always smacks a bit of I, nor too much indulgence. That, too, is a Middle Way.

In our own cultural and religious background we have a tremendous symbol of what this willingly suffering it out with open eyes points to and means in living and subjective form – and not just as a story that happened long ago. Christ hanging on the cross, his arms stretched out, open, completely defenceless and totally vulnerable, the gall, the pain, the shame, and the lance piercing the heart. Have we ever given a thought to what this actually points to? It is said that he did it for us, to show the Way. For this is the attitude of meekly suffering it through, and out. The heart must break; the rigid crust of I that clutches the soft heart in an iron grip, must break. Only then is the heart liberated, and after a descent into the nethermost, I-less, regions it rises again as from the dead. Nothing can be said about that. It is a mystery for which there is no explanation, only first-hand experience.

This attitude, passive, gentle, without resistance, avoiding nothing, willing, open, this is required in the training and is produced by it, nurtured by it, fostered and furthered by it, until it ripens. I have nothing to do with it, for me it is totally passive. But, at the same time, I also have an active role which is equally important, and without which nothing can happen. The suffering it out meekly is one side of the coin which in itself is not productive of a real change. My active role is doing and continuing to do the daily chores smoothly and efficiently, never stopping on account of my suffering, carrying on while, metaphorically, hanging on the cross. This double action is all important for the forging, acting as anvil and hammer in the process.

It is also said that our individual crosses just fit us. If I, arbitrarily or with zealous intention, lay on more, I upset the balance, for that is again 'as it suits me'. Even my best intentions are as I want it, and in that is already the unwillingness to take things as they come.

A Zen story makes this point still clearer. A man hangs over a sheer cliff, gripping one big root with one hand for dear life. The other arm and both his feet already dangle over the abyss. Can he open his hand and let go? Allow himself to fall? For that is what he is asked to do in the training.

The Zen Way is not something arbitrarily concocted; it follows the natural pattern. Life, too, hangs us on that cliff when we feel with every fibre that this only is what we want and nothing else is really important. Does this also give us a further inkling of why we hang on the great? When all our little wants and appetites and lusts seem trivial and only one thing matters? This is that strong single root to which we cling, and it means more to us than our own life. Many lives have been laid down, willingly, for the sake of holding on to that root. Nor is that wrong, but the seeing clearly matters even more,

Yes, Life, too, hangs us on that cliff at least a few times. But nothing makes us realise that we need to let go of that root – nor do I have the strength to open the hand and let go. In a way, it could also be said that the one thing that matters more to me than I, the overwhelming want and/or fear is just that I need to give up, to find the heart.

What the Zen Way does is to hang us on that cliff, by whittling away the little things we cling to in the course of the training, or, more accurately, by combining them like so many threads into one strong rope that holds and binds us in that precarious position on the cliff. That much, Life does, too, to give us the chance, as it were. But the Zen Way has also opened our eyes to see, and to dare to see, where we are and to understand what we have to do, and given us the strength to do it.

But we ourselves must open the clutching fist and actually let go. No Way can do this for us; only we can open the fist – and fall. Again, into the nethermost regions; to use the bull-herding analogy, the 'man has vanished'. He has fallen 'into the origin, back to the source', from where he re-emerges, 'comes back to the market with bliss-bestowing hands'.

The Great Death has been died and now there is nothing but Life. This Life has become conscious of itself, awakened, and sees clearly with the single eye the manifold forms of Life, which blindly struggle, blindly suffer, fulfilling the pattern of what is, shaping itself on the woof and warp of coming to be and ceasing to be – formation, transformation – striving to see, out of the original darkness.

In the Awakened, this wisdom-knowledge, this insight, is the other side of the warmth that flows from his liberated heart as Love, and what his heart and hands touch is quickened. All flowers turn to the sun.

This is the Practice in Daily Life, or Acceptance Practice: an attitude of service, of consideration for what is. It is a slow process of ripening, of becoming whole. Though there is nothing dramatic about it, it entails the labours and birth-pangs attendant on all 'coming to be'. Thus it is productive of a true change in the trainee which is irreversible. It cannot be stressed too much or too often that this practice must be undertaken and carried out voluntarily, with full acceptance and effort, in full awareness and with willing participation. A mere going through the forms of it, a mechanical application, will produce nothing. Validly done, it is a liberating of the heart, and a restructuring of the whole personality, through which the warmth of the heart is released.

Zazen, 'sitting meditation', is the other side to Acceptance, or the Practice in Daily Life; without the latter, the former is sterile. Practice in Daily Life is like one leg with which to walk the Zen Way; the other leg, without which there can be no walking, is Zazen. Hence it is a fallacy to believe or to hope that Zazen alone, without the Daily Life Practice, is fruitful or will change one, preferably will waft one out of one's difficulties, problems and resistances. To try to escape into meditation in order to avoid the difficult task of taming the bull of one's emotionality, the wild aspect of one's heart connected with I, is at best useless, can be dangerous, but is very human and such attempts have accompanied the Zen school right from the beginning.

Hui Neng already warns against quiet sitting only. A few generations after him we have a classical story on the same theme:

a very diligent young monk used every spare moment of his time to do Zazen. His Master noticed the honesty and persever-ance of his endeavour, and to help him, one day when the young monk was 'sitting Zen' in a corner of the yard, the Master picked up a brick, sat himself down beside the monk and rubbing the brick with the palm of his hand, asked the monk, 'What are you doing?' 'I am trying to become a Buddha,' was the hopeful reply, then noticing the Master rubbing the brick, the monk asked, 'But, Master, what are you doing?' 'I am making a mirror,' said the Master. 'Surely no amount of rubbing will make a brick into a mirror,' exclaimed the astonished monk. 'And no amount of sitting will make a clod into a Buddha,' stated the Master.

Truly, the clod that I am can only be restructured, trans-formed, with the Practice in Daily Life. Then why Zazen? Zazen clears the sight. Through Zazen we learn to see clearly, to acquire that genuine insight of which Master Rinzai says that it is the one thing the Zen student needs to have. But without the Practice in Daily Life, the acceptance of one's own emotional reactions and suffering them through, Zazen remains blind. Both balance and complement each other. What is worked in the one is made clear, 'seen into' by the other. Hence genuine insight comes as hindsight from experience.

With a totally untamed bull, with an overweening I suddenly shut up, all contacts with the outside cut, all usual distractions to the senses taken away, 'the inner film' begins to roll, for nature abhors a vacuum. Visions and hallucinations occur, as sense deprivation tests carried out in the United States show beyond doubt. They were carried out with hand-picked post-graduate student volunteers, alone in dark, soundproof rooms, floating in body-temperature liquid to prevent sense of touch.

And there is also the growing number of lone sailors, who testify that what they find hardest to contend with is not storm or tempest, for then there is still something to do and their reactions are directed outwards, but the long, calm spells – these they really fear because nothing happens and there is nothing to do, nothing to react to or against; then the inner film takes over and reality becomes tenuous. A man can be swallowed by it.

I am impatient and likely to rush hot-headed after everything that promises the fulfilment of what I want. But being hot-headed is being blind. Zazen is a live, training process and not a soulless, mechanical method; it is not a kind of *deus ex machina,* not just a hopeful attempt at blotting myself out, to find myself wafted miraculously on to another shore with no more suffering and no more problems. I tend to get carried away by such hopes of wonderful happenings and take the inner film all too easily as the 'fruits of Zazen'. The mistake could not be greater. As a recent Zen Master said with regard to this inner wonder-word: 'And even if you see the Buddha himself riding towards you on a white elephant, you are 1,000 miles off course.'

Nor is Zazen a safety island where one can avoid the trials and tribulations of our daily life. That is a gross misuse which leads rather back than forward and turns us into escapists. Master Hakuin says of this empty emptiness that it is 'sitting in a cave filled with the slime of one's self-accredited achievement'.

In the West we have lost our own spiritual tradition. So we do well to admit our total ignorance and approach meditation, all forms of it, circumspectly and carefully, and at the least with a sense of reverence. The latter is the right attitude with which to undertake it. If we rush at it greedily, we are likely to fall into a trendy-ism which does not succour; there are plenty such about. All is not gold that glitters. The present-day vogue for either 'blotting out', or for the 'highs' of the inner life, makes it even more imperative to approach with care.

Zazen cannot be 'explained'. Understanding comes by the practice of it, and by the experience of doing it. This is what experience means, not in the sense of 'experience' as it is misunderstood and equated with an emotional 'high'. It is just this misunderstanding that has led to the erroneous equation of 'experience' equals a psychedelic, drug-induced or any other type of 'high'. As a matter of fact, it is just the opposite of this.

Zen experience may be taken in the sense of familiarity with, and acquired skill in handling something: like typing, or cooking, to use analogies from ordinary, daily life. Cooking is a good example, because the inexperienced cook finds it quite difficult to follow a cookbook which is addressed to the more experienced cook familiar with terminology such as 'a knob of butter' or 'cook in moderate oven until done'.

Zazen instructions are rather like these cookery books. They are manuals to guide and remind the meditator and help him to continue. They are of little use to start with, as too much is unknown.

There is no magic in the integral calculus, and a child just learning the multiplication table has the intellect to understand it but as yet has insufficient expertise and knowledge of mathematics to follow the explanation. Thus the child merely becomes confused by an attempt to do so, and thinks it difficult and beyond his grasp. If he just continues the usual course in mathematics he will quite naturally come to an understanding of it.

The same applies to Zazen or any meditation training. Practice is necessary, and after that it begins to look quite different from what I thought, hoped or imagined. That is one of the many early difficulties, for if the training turns out differently from what I fondly imagined, I may turn away from it and give it up. Hence the root of faith, together with the root of doubt, and the indomitable, almost fierce courage, which are said to be essential to start and carry out this training.

One cannot learn to meditate head-on; that which wants to learn is in the way. It can only be tackled in a round-about way. Sitting in a position that is likely to induce a calm state: a firm base triangle, as a camera is put on a tripod for the stability necessary for long exposure. This is achieved by placing a large flat cushion on the floor to give support and putting a smaller one on it to actually sit upon, and resting the knees firmly on the flat cushion. This triangular base gives the firm support needed. If the body is unstable, the mind wobbles too. On this base triangle is set the upper triangle of shoulders and spine with the small of the back arched so that the skeletal structure carries itself without muscle strain. The head is balanced on top, as the apex of this triangle. In front the nose and navel are in a straight line, and sideways, the ears, shoulders and hips are also in line.

Headaches are the result of incorrect posture; slumping and hanging the head forward tires and cramps the shoulder and neck muscles. When this stable position is achieved, it creates the most favourable condition for calming the heart. The exercise in concentration is to count the breath in its natural rhythm. Exhalations only are counted from one to ten. If thoughts interfere, one starts again from one, without being side-tracked into wondering how far one had counted. The breathing is not forced and the stress is laid on the counting rather than on the breathing.

From the very beginning it is important to put as much effort into the counting as one can muster. But it has to be 'right' effort – not in the sense of 'I am now sitting, I am counting, I am concentrating', but a total giving oneself over to the counting, going into it and losing oneself in it. It is best described as mentally going forward to meet the count and mingling with it.

The eyes are slightly open, which helps alertness and awareness and also effectively prevents the starting of the inner film. Hands are supported on the lap with either the thumbs supporting each other or the hands gripping one another – the latter is easier for the beginner. The hands or arms should be sufficiently supported; dangling arms will pull the shoulders forward, with backaches inevitably resulting from the consequent muscle strain. For a beginner there are many questions about what to do but the few things that really need to be done are easily kept in mind: it is important that the hands should be well gripped or the thumbs well braced – this preserves muscle-tone and alertness. Woolly-headedness or day-dreaming is not Zazen.

A Japanese proverb says: 'Better than learning it, get used to it.' What is only in the head does not cut any ice in practice. Perseverance in the practice, getting used to it, answers most questions. But occasional checks are useful, for quite unbeknown to oneself one can easily fall into inconducive habits which, once acquired, are extremely difficult to get rid of. In the beginning great care is important. Don't hurry hopefully to some imagined goal.

Obstacles arise in the course of Zazen practice, and need to be worked through. Among the usual ones, the first is that the mere counting soon becomes very boring and the bull wants greener pastures to disport itself in. 'Why, this is ridiculous, of course I can count; silly exercise for muddle-headed people, but surely not for me! I can do better than that; I am no longer in the kindergarten. Why can't I have a real subject for meditation. How well I could work on it and make progress instead of this soul-destroying counting which is more likely to make me into a robot.' Thus real doubt begins to raise its head: 'Is it wise?'

This involves a real struggle and unless some experience with the Daily Life Practice has given one extra strength and understanding, one is likely to give up at this hurdle, either for good, or to go in search for a 'better' method or teacher.

Daily Life Practice and Zazen Training are intricately connected, complementing each other; one without the other is not likely to lead to clarity, only to greater confusion.

However, by persevering and by pressing on patiently, this hurdle is suffered through. In this training it is best not to think of overcoming or conquering but only of suffering through. And other obstacles are in store, which may appear one by one or else jumbled together. Having suffered through the resistance against the boring counting, an easier stretch now follows in which either sleepiness or withdrawal into what the old texts call the empty emptiness may occur. In short, the alertness sags. Strength to get through these obstacles accrues from the Daily Life Practice, which helps us to endure and function smoothly in circumstances which I resist. Thus these obstacles are also worked through, at least to some extent. Balance is essential; if working through these obstacles becomes unduly difficult, for whatever reasons, the cause is in the Daily Life Practice and needs to be remedied there. It cannot be emphasised strongly enough that meditation without a framework of daily discipline does not bear fruit.

If a balance is kept in the practice, if Zazen is taken as part of that overall Daily Life Practice, and not something special and apart from it, there will be moments when one jerks out from some state, having lost the count not by inattention or sleepiness, but simply by vanishing into depth. This in itself is of no interest, for I am not, and cannot be, aware of this. But on coming out of it one is, just for a split second at first, without the usual I-bias, hence seeing clearly. Of course, one cannot hold this seeing, because I have again become self-conscious; and wishing to hold it or thinking about it drives it away. The best course is patiently to persevere with the practice, which will lengthen and deepen these moments until one becomes more and more accustomed to them. This quiet awareness, with the mirror wiped clean as it emerges from the depth, is the real meditation. It takes long practice and is an absence of the I that I know.

It is also in this real meditation that one can look at one's problems without I-bias; in this clear seeing, solutions present themselves which then need to be put into practice in one's everyday life. Finally, as one is really becoming one with this state, it holds not only on the meditation cushion. As an attitude it begins to pervade one's daily activities until it becomes one's ordinary way of life.

A useful experiment is to become aware of the process of falling asleep. With practice, the stages of the process can be differentiated. I cannot fall asleep. We all know the jolt when we drop off too quickly because we are yet too strong to 'let go'. But normally this happens smoothly, and at the moment of drop-off a wide, warm security opens, intimate and close, and a joyful sinking into it – home, origin. It happens every night.

We need to go home to relax and to be refreshed, to get out of the day-garment of I, and draw new strength from the source.

If there is too much emphasis on I, I become overwrought, thus alienated from 'home'. We suffer from insomnia, and instead of applying ourselves to redress the imbalance, we swallow sleeping pills to blot ourselves out. For in order to live we must have rest from I.

No talk about the Zen Way is complete without mentioning death. If we learn to be fully alive, we also learn to die fully. Along the Zen Way, I lose my fear of extinction. Through meditation there takes place a habituation in that I-less place, not just as in sleep which we all know, but in awareness. Death, too, leads back into that I-less place, and with this awareness death is seen as a fulfilment. The prodigal son has returned home.

In the Acceptance Practice in Daily Life we have learned to take and to make use of all that comes. A good thing is gratefully enjoyed while it lasts and is not clung to when it goes; and a difficult thing is embraced as good practice and gratefully made use of rather than avoided and rejected. Nothing is refused; all is lived and learned from. I become ever softer, the way home ever clearer, the bull now carries the man. No unlived life piles up as threat and fear.

The winds of passion whip up into waves the smooth surface of the living, breathing ocean. One individual wave is ephemeral, short-lived, trampled upon by the wave behind, itself trampling on the one in front, hemmed in and interfered with by the waves on either side. Were such a single wave conscious of itself, knowing that it soon must go down, trying to hold its own against all the others, wouldn't it scream with fear and desperation as, bruised and mutilated, it plunges down into the depth? But were this single wave aware that whether up or down it is nothing but ocean, as indeed are all the other waves, would there be the same problems, the same fear? When the winds of passion have blown themselves out, there is nothing but the living ocean. Oh yes, death is a fulfilment. We approach this in our practice of the Zen Way and become aware of it in and by meditation.

Death today is hedged around by fear. In newspapers and news broadcasts we are daily regaled by the violence of death which increases our fear. We no longer die naturally at home, nor do we normally keep our relatives at home or are near them when they die. We no longer see nor are familiar with dying, and knowing only of the violence we are afraid and fight death. We know nothing of the natural acceptance of death when it comes close, nothing of the majesty and dignity of Death. Indeed, we have estranged ourselves from the home we long for. We have robbed ourselves of our inheritance and cannot live fully because, no longer seeing the dignity of a dead face, we dare not look at the face of Death and so cannot die fully.

As a child, I lived in a remote country area. People died at home and though they were certainly not saints, living close to nature they knew when death drew near. A householder put his house in order, often arranged for his own funeral down to what food should be served and how much beer and wine should be provided for the veterans, for the fire brigade and all who would follow the coffin and afterwards sit down to the meal. Then, having settled his worldly affairs, surrounded by his family, and having made his peace with God, he could go with death peacefully and in trust. Such a person's dead face is stamped with the peace and the majesty of Death. And the wake allows time for this awareness, lifting the personal grief to what is 'grave and constant' in human experience.

We read in the Zen texts of the Masters knowing that their end is drawing near and writing their farewell poem while looking into the face of Death. This evoked in me childhood memories of how the villagers also faced death, and indeed, when later there was a little hospital in a nearby town, the ambulance was not only busy bringing people to it, but it also carried the dying home. The doctor did not tell them; they knew themselves and would ask to be brought back home to die – a request that was never refused.

Shortly before leaving Japan, I mentioned this to the Master under whom I was training; he nodded. 'Things like these you should tell people when you return'.

In the Acceptance Practice in Daily Life, we also learn the joy of obedience. And the far-reaching ramifications of it. An I with strong desires can never see clearly because the desires blind and delude. This applies not only to the crude appetites but to any strong desires or aversions, however altruistic or seemingly so. Hence the doctrine of No-I. Hence the training discipline to wean I from the emphasis on myself and of any opinions. I am forever separate, forever on the defensive, forever wanting because of my lack of security, and so, forever afraid. Liberation is not from what I do not like so that I can do what I like. Acceptance and endurance of what I do not like weaken I and effect a transformation of the emotional energy. This is deliverance from I and my blinkered, limited sight; this naturally opens to the full, clear seeing, and the warmth and joy inherent in the human heart. If I am out of the way, what is, becomes apparent. I and my fears topple over in the deepest seat of consciousness; what I used to see as fear is now perceived as the boundless love of the heart in which 'I' and 'other' both vanish.

The first insights are relatively easy but the real transformations, which last and become one's attitude in daily life, require long and patient practice, and a sincere reverence without which nothing can be accomplished.

In this clear seeing there is no judgement. But since the seeing is clear, there is certainly a seeing of distinctions. The 'all is the same' concept leads back into basic ignorance, the lack of inner strength and concomitant emotionality.

Clear seeing is the end of fear and disease in the fullness of the heart; it is accompanied by joy and gratitude. This is the goal of the Zen Way. And with it, we come back to the basic Buddhist teachings, for surely a Way that leads out of suffering is bound to end up in joy. Such is the basic message of Buddhism. And it is for everyone who feels inclined to practise it, now as then.

CONCLUSIONS

As a Way of training, the Zen Way has always been open to all who wished to tread it and were prepared to make the relevant effort. Both in China and Japan it counted Emperors and statesmen as well as artists of great renown among its followers. Professional soldiers took to it to overcome the fear of death and to give them strength. All kinds of lay people, both men and women, have found their inherent talents and creativity in it, and as an attitude to life it has deeply influenced Far Eastern art and culture. However, as a Way of training it has always been in the hands of 'professionals' who have run places for this training to ground the trainees in this life, either to experience the atmosphere at first for a few days, or for a few weeks or months, or for years of training. As a school it insists that proven guides be available for trainees. In more than 1,000 years of its existence it has come to know of human endeavour and human potential, and also of human difficulties, human weakness, and human folly, but above all of the recurrent obstacles that beset the path; and it has come to learn how to work through them and out of them. To do this without getting lost a guide is needed on this path. But the trainee must walk it himself.

If the Zen Way is to come to the West such training places will be needed and will emerge. And if it is to lead into the future, they will be run by guides who have themselves absorbed the training of the Zen Way. It is a way of life; but first and foremost it is a religious way.

To repeat, the Zen Way is not different or apart from the Buddhist Way, which is the Buddha's Way. As a school, it calls itself the Buddha Heart School. The Buddha was a man who by his own perseverance and effort found the Way to the Heart, the human heart, one's very own. He himself realised that this Way was not new, but that he had only rediscovered an ancient path, leading to an ancient city. Truly, the Zen Way is as old as that Heart itself, and so is always discoverable, however overgrown or forgotten it may have become.

This Heart is not the possession of the Zen School. And though the Zen School has kept alive one specific Way to it, to be trodden by the indomitable, a Way which is perhaps straighter than most, it is certainly not the only Way. The Zen School is well aware of this and holds that there is the Zen of the ordinary man, the 'peasant who uses it every day but does not know it'; there is the Zen of 'other ways', of other religious traditions; there is the Zen of the various Buddhist Schools, and there is the Zen of the Zen Way. It could not be said fairer.

The Zen Way is a demanding way, but it leads to the depths, to the light of clearly seeing what is when the veil is rent, and to the warmth of heart that touches and engenders growth. Thus it is a way of joyful service to all beings. As to the service, a contemporary Zen Master said that there is no end to it. This must be so, for it stretches into the future towards an end of suffering and for the peace of all beings.

At this the heart bows in gratitude, to the guides, the long line of patriarchs through the generations, and to that first guide whom all have followed, the Buddha, the All-Enlightened, the All-Compassionate One. It is a living chain. And so to the link that was instrumental in shaping or guiding a heart on this

Way, there goes a gratitude which cannot be repaid and makes that heart flow over; nine prostrations to the teacher – and may the warmth thus released touch other hearts and incite them to tread the Way towards it.

FURTHER READING

Mainstream Buddhism. Eric Cheetham, Booklets 1-4,
The Buddhist Society, London, 1986-1988.

The Development of Chinese Zen. Heinrich Dumoulin
& Ruth Sasaki, The First Zen Institute of America, 1953.

The Essentials of Buddhist Philosophy. Junjiro Takakusu,
University Press Hawaii, 1947.

Mahayana Buddhism. Paul Williams, Routledge
& Kegan Paul, 1989.

A First Zen Reader. Trevor Leggett, Tuttle, 1960.

The Tiger's Cave (Second Zen Reader). Trevor Leggett,
Rider, 1964.

Zen Action, Zen Person. T P Kasulis, University Press
Hawaii, 1981.

THE ZEN CENTRE

The Zen Centre is a registered charity with the object of encouraging the practice and study of Zen Buddhism. It offers a structured training programme both at its own premises and at the Buddhist Society, 58 Eccleston Square, London, SW1V 1PH.

Other Zen Centre Publications:
Gentling the Bull by Myokyo-ni
Pointers to Insight by Soko Roshi
The Ceasing of Notions by Soko Roshi
The Bull and His Herdsman by Otsu Roshi

Also available:
Zen Traces, quarterly magazine.
Introducing Buddhism, pamphlet.

Enquiries in writing to:
The Zen Centre
58 Marlborough Place
London NW8 0PL